THE ISLAMIC FINANCE AND THE *Riba*

Their Fundamental
Nature and
Intellectual Basis

Revised Edition

ZUBAIR KAREEM

Copyright 2021 by Zubair Kareem

All rights reserved.

No part of this book may be reproduced in any form or by any electronic or mechanical means including information storage and retrieval systems, except in the case of brief quotations embodied in critical articles or reviews – without permission in writing from its publisher.

To contact the author, email:
BCAL2013@yahoo.com

Paperback ISBN#: 9798770964998
Hardcover ISBN#: 9798770967814

Cover and interior design:
Deborah Perdue
https:illuminationgraphics.com

Dedication

The South Hadley *Halqah*

My teachers
My friends
And
To my family

Near and far

But, especially,
To the next generation of Muslims
In the USA

Contents

Preface vii
Chapter 1. Introduction 1
Chapter 2. Intellectual Foundation of Islam 7
Chapter 3. Islamic Thought Process 13
Chapter 4. Why Was an Opinion Always Needed? 21
Chapter 5. Interpretation or Translation of the Quran 29
Chapter 6. The Hadith of the Prophet SAW 41
Chapter 7. The Concept of Internal Consistency 51
Chapter 8. Formal Difference of Opinion in Islam 57
Chapter 9. The Concept of Juristic Analysis 69
Chapter 10. Riba in Ancient Civilizations
            and Previous Scriptures 73
Chapter 11. What Was in the Quran About Riba? 79
Chapter 12. Riba and Finance in the Hadith Literature 97
Chapter 13. Riba In Islam, its Basis and Nature 123
Chapter 14. The Rules of Islamic Finance 139
Chapter 15. Islamic Finance in Real Life, or
            Its Practical Implications 159
Chapter 16. Islamic Economy and
            Corporate Governance 247
Chapter 17. The Conclusion 275

Preface

It is an honor for me to present the revised edition of this book. Main purpose for this revision was to correct some errors, and some clarification of thought. In addition, I added a chapter on the Islamic version of economy, and corporate governance, a subject requiring much more attention in Islamic societies. In addition to my previous complements, I am particularly grateful to Mr. Khawar Saeed, a true intellect with multiple literary talents. He has done a tremendous favor to me by translating the first edition of this book in Urdu. In addition, he provided many useful edits for this edition. May Allah SWT raise his ranks in this world and the hereafter.

For someone interested in the main subject of this book, the *Riba*, and not interested in reading, I have recorded some lectures, which are available at my YouTube channel, https://WWW.youtube.com/@zubairkareem/videos.

CHAPTER 1

Introduction

In recent times, finance, a more comprehensive English word for the monetary side of trading and business, has become an integral part of modern-day living. Islam allows and encourages business but with certain restrictions and prohibitions. These restrictions and prohibitions are the impetus for a set of rules and regulations giving rise to the concept of "Islamic finance". In this essay, I address general principles of Islamic finance, with emphasis on Riba. I do not address how one should do business or what might be the "Islamic" business model. Islam allows people to find a way for business of their liking. The purpose of Islamic financial rules and regulations is to provide some controls and define certain restrictions and limits. Within these boundaries and following these rules, one is free to undertake any business venture.

Despite its complex nature, my purpose undertaking this project is to discuss and explain Islamic financial principles, and especially Riba, in a relatively simple and straightforward manner. My particular interest is the fundamental religious basis of financial rules and injunctions. It is my observation that most Muslims lack a deeper understanding of basic intellectual principles of Islam, especially when they apply to practical matters like business. Most simply follow a certain way, as their ancestors did. This approach might be one of the reasons for lack of full understanding of the concept of Riba, and its application in their personal lives, or the society et large. For this reason, a significant part of the book is devoted to this issue, with a hope that it might help to improve basic Islamic understandings for anyone new to Islam or living in it for decades.

A large part of the book is dedicated to explaining the intellectual foundation of Islam, with a brief outline of the history of its thought processes. I believe this is important before going into the discussion of a matter as practical and complex as finance or the Riba. Also important is to mention and define the diversity of opinion within Muslim scholarship. Difference of opinion within the community existed from early on and was not just because of its large size. It was of multiple types, and in this book, it is discussed in reference to Finance and the Riba.

The next two chapters are about the status of the Quran and the Hadith in Islamic thought process. A brief chapter is about the concept of Riba in pre-Islamic religions, especially Judaism and Christianity. In the following chapter are references about the Riba in the Quran, which follow a similar chapter on the references about the Riba and finance in the Hadith. A chapter is dedicated to the principles underlying

Chapter 1 – Introduction

the rules of Riba. Finally, I try to present a practical and common-sense approach of understanding the Riba, and the fundamentals of Islamic finance.

This writing is meant for an average American or an English-speaking Muslim or a layperson, not for a religious scholar or an academic of Islamic finance. It is also not intended for either the so-called "Sunnis" or the "Shias;" it is for all Muslims, and anyone else interested in Islam. But it is for a person with an open, fair, and inquisitive mind. For a Muslim, who feels more comfortable just following an established practice or an Imam, without asking any questions, certain elements of this writing may provoke anxiety and a feeling of doubt. If that is the case, my recommendation is to take the next best step by researching the original material, i.e., the Quran and the books of the Prophet's Sunnah and the Hadith literature, the basis of all religious opinions in Islam.

Arabic is not my primary or even secondary language. I learned a part of it primarily to have better understanding of the Quran and the Hadith. I acknowledged that understanding of the Quran and the Hadith for a person like me may not match the understanding of a native speaker of the Quranic Arabic. Additionally, despite good amount of translated material available for an English speaking or English understanding person in these days, there still is a large amount of scholarly work of early generations that has either not been translated or is not easily available. I hope that as larger Islamic academic institutions are established in the U. S. A. and other English-speaking countries, this long overdue task might be undertaken. In spite of these limitations, I believe enough material is available for research, and to discuss this subject matter.

Multiple translations of the Quran are available, and I reviewed many, the list is provided in the relevant chapter. I found some translations to be, in literal terms, somewhat more representative of the words of the Quran than others. I also found that some translations were easier to comprehend than others. In terms of overall authenticity of translation, in spite of its use of old-fashioned English language, I found Abdullah Yusuf Ali's translation (may Allah SWT accept his effort), The Meaning of the Holy Quran, surpassing others. On the other hand, the Meaning of the Noble Quran by Dr. M. Taqiuddin Al-Hilali & Dr. M. Muhsin Khan's (may Allah SWT accept their effort) was one of the easier to understand. For most Quranic references, I included these two translations, except the chapter specifically about the Quran where I added three more. The purpose was to expose the reader to a variety of translations, which were all well respected in their own account, but did provide subtle difference of opinion and approach.

As far as the Hadith literature is concerned, main books of Hadith were listed. Looking at the list, one wonders if all authors were documenting the same thing, why was there a need for repeated effort? There seemed to be two explanations: a. Just like any other science, more than one or two persons were working on this task around the same time frame, in different geographical locations or religious circle of influence, and b. Some of the later work seemed to have been done for a different purpose, trying to provide an alternate view instead of emphasis on documentation. For this work, I reviewed the following five books of the Hadith: Al-Muwatta, Sahih Al-Bukhari, Sahih Muslim, Sunan Abu Dawud, and Sunan Ibn Majah.

Chapter 1 – Introduction

For a believer, talking and especially writing about religious matters is a burdensome task. Its repercussions, which carries tremendous responsibility, is clearly explained in the Quran:

The Quran, An-Nisa, ayah 85 (Al-Quran 4:85):

> "Whoever recommends and helps a good cause becomes a partner therein: and whoever recommends and helps an evil cause, shares in its burden: and Allah hath power over all things." Ali.

> "Whoever intercedes for a good cause will have the reward thereof, and whosoever intercedes for an evil cause will have a share in its burden. And Allah is Ever All-Able to do (and also an All-Witness to) everything." Al-Hilali & Khan.

The mistakes you may find in the reference section, its translation, or within my commentary of a subject matter are all mine. I pray to Allah SWT for forgiveness and request His specially Mercy. I hope that with His blessing this writing may help readers clarify thinking about this complex practical subject.

There are many people contributing to this effort, mostly indirectly, but many provided direct and very important help. I am thankful to my dear brothers, friends, and teachers Imam Wissam Abdel Baki, Khalid Al-Zamzamy, and Osama Jalal who helped me understand some Arabic words and expressions. I am especially indebted to Khawaja Mohammad Yusuf and his daughter Tayyaba Chaudhary (the first edition) for the editing work, performing it timely and graciously. Members of our local

South Hadley Halqah inspired me to undertake this project, and I am thankful for their time, effort, and grace. I am thankful to my friends, who sometimes ask difficult questions. Finally, my special gratitude is to my family, my wife and my children, and my brother Khalid Mahmood, a constant source of stimulation and inspiration. May Allah SWT provide all of them from His special Mercy.

CHAPTER 2

Intellectual Foundation of Islam

Before addressing a specific issue like the Islamic finance, it may be useful to review some of the fundamental intellectual concepts of Islam. Understanding of these concepts is the key to understand rules, regulations, and recommendations in Islam. For the subject of the Islamic finance, understanding of the intellectual foundation of Islam is essential. The following outline is designed to help understand its underpinning:

The Principle
    The Quran, the book of Allah SWT

The Manual
    The *Sunnah* and the *Hadith* of the Prophet Muhammad SAW (what he taught, did, recommended, stated, approved, disapproved, or did not prohibit)

The Opinions
The First 4 Caliphs RA (*rahmatullah alaihay*)
The Major Schools of thought
The Scholars
Miscellaneous, e.g., the local Imam

Islam's intellectual base primarily is the Quran. The Quran mentions that the Prophet Muhammad SAW followed the same religion as all previous prophets of Allah SWT, starting with Prophet Adam, AS (*Allah salaam*). Islam, in the manner known to us, started with the prophethood of Muhammad SAW. Its first message was revealed as the first word of the Quran. The Quran was slowly and methodically revealed to the Prophet during the next 23 years. Besides many other details, it provided the basic principles of Islam. It also provided an outline of some of the rules of Islamic finance. Further details are based upon how the Prophet SAW conducted financial matters, and what he stated, clarified, approved, or disapproved. He was the final arbiter of interpretation of the Quran, and any other religious matter. Instructions to the believers are straightforward and explicit, as elaborated in the following two *ayat:*

The Quran, Al-Ahzab, *ayah* 36 (Al-Quran 33:36)
"It is not fitting for a Believer, man or woman, when a matter has been decided by Allah and His Messenger, to have any option about their decision: if anyone disobeys Allah and His Messenger he is indeed on a clearly wrong path." Ali.

"It is not for a believer, man or woman, when Allah and His Messenger have decreed a matter that they should have any option in their decision. And whoever disobeys Allah and His

Messenger, he has indeed strayed into a plain error." Al-Hilali and Khan.

The Quran, Al-Hashr, *ayah* 7 (Al-Quran 59:7)
" . . . so take what the Messenger assigns to you, and deny yourselves that which he withholds from you. And fear Allah . . . " Ali.
" . . . and whatsoever the Messenger (Muhammad SAW) gives you, take it, and whatsoever he forbids you, abstain (from it), & fear Allah . . . " Al-Hilali and Khan.

The Quran, An-Nisa, *ayah* 65 (Al-Quran 4:65)
"But no, by thy Lord, they can have no (real) Faith, until they make thee judge in all disputes between them, and find in their souls no resistance against thy decisions, but accept them with the fullest conviction." Ali.

"But no, by your Lord, they can have no Faith, until they make you (O Muhammad SAW) judge in all disputes between them, and find in themselves no resistance against your decisions, and accept (them) with full submission." Al-Hilali & Khan.

The relationship of the Quran to the *Hadith* of the Prophet SAW is somewhat like the relationship a modern-day constitution of a country might have with its governing rules and by-laws. The purpose of the constitution is to outline the fundamental principles, based upon which rules and regulations are designed, and then practiced. The Prophet's life was a practical manifestation of the principles outlined in the Quran, as stated by his beloved wife Ayesha, may Allah SWT be pleased with her; when someone asked her about him or his character, she answered, "Haven't you read the Quran?"

In a way, the Prophet's life, in the form of his *Seerah* (biography), and the *Hadith* literature, is a manual for us to consult for anything about religion or the life in general. Aside from this similarity, the Quran also differs from a constitution in critical manner. Constitutions are man-made and are technically changeable or revocable; the Quran is from Allah SWT, and is permanent, unalterable, and irrevocable. Also, by stating that the Prophet's life reflected the Quran, it is understood that his opinion on any matter was to provide interpretation of what was stated in the Quran, and not a separate or parallel view.

This analogy might also help to understand another aspect of the Quran and the Prophet SAW. Some people have taken the position that they may accept anything mentioned in the Quran but for whatever reason, nothing else. This approach is somewhat like stating that one may accept anything written in the constitution of a country but not any of its regulations, laws and traditions, an approach that will be impractical to say the least. Of course, one may review a regulation or a law, which is not an uncommon practice, to make sure it follows the principles outlined in the constitution. Similarly, in principle, there shall not be any conflict in our understanding of what is stated in the Quran and documented in the *Sunnah* and the *Hadith* of the Prophet SAW. In case of any apparent conflict, one shall spend more time and effort to research the original material (the Quran, the *Hadith*, and the *Seerah*) and consult proper scholars for clarification and better understanding.

Finally, it is an important reminder that the Quran and the Islam we practice and are aware of came to us through the beloved Prophet Muhammad SAW; there is literally no Islam without him.

CHAPTER 3

ISLAMIC THOUGHT PROCESS

Human life is in evolution resulting in constant flow of new issues requiring Islamic clarification, i.e., how to address them according to the Islamic principles. This process of requiring expert religious opinion started early on. To understand this historical process, how it came into being, how it continues to evolve, and in which direction it may go in the future, the following scheme may help. In this scheme the history of Islamic thought process is arbitrarily divided in different phases:

Phases of Islamic Thought Process

- Phase I (Foundational Phase)
  - Life of the Prophet SAW
  - Until 11 AH (632 CE)
  - **Clarifying authority: The Prophet SAW**

- Phase II (Formative Phase)
  - First 4 caliphs

- 11 AH to around 40 AH (632-660 CE)
- **Clarifying authority: The Caliph**

- Phase III (Seminal Phase)
  - About 40 AH to around 595 AH (660-1198 CE)
  - **Clarifying authority: Many**

- Phase IV (Static Phase)
  - About 595 AH to 1421 AH (1198-2000 CE)
  - **Clarifying authority: Too many**

- Phase V (Revival Phase)
  - About 1420 AH (2000 CE) onwards
  - **Clarifying authority: Too many**

The 1st phase of Islamic thought process started with the first revelation of the Quran and the pronouncement of the Prophet Muhammad SAW as the messenger of Allah SWT. It lasted until the Prophet SAW passed away, 11 years after he migrated (the *Hijra*) to Madinah. This was the foundational and the most important phase of Islam. The Quran was revealed to the Prophet during this phase. In practical terms, the Prophet provided an example of how to live a Muslim life. He personally taught and guided Muslims on religious and related practical matters. They had direct access to his authority, which, on any religious matter, was ultimate and final.

The 2nd historical phase started after the Prophet SAW passed away. For about next three decades, during the caliphate of the first four caliphs, the caliph was ultimately responsible for any clarification in religious matters, or any issue related to the Islamic law. All these four caliphs, may Allah SWT be pleased with them,

Chapter 3 – Islamic Thought Processes

had spent a large part of their life with the Prophet, and they were from his closest associates and friends. Going through historical records of that period one could fathom that any opinion they provided was based upon the principles outlined in the Quran, and the sayings and the ways of the Prophet SAW. Despite that, it is incorrect to state that there was no difference of opinion or disagreement, sometimes even quite serious and devastating for the community, during this phase. But overall, and in relative terms, there was a consensus within the Muslim community.

The 3rd historical phase started after passing of the fourth caliph, *Hazrat* Ali ibn Abi Talib, may Allah SWT be please with him, in the year 661 AD, or 40 AH. After his passing, there were multiple socio-political and religious factors leading to the loss of consensus within the larger Muslim society. These differences ultimately led to at least some variations in intellectual understanding of religion, including interpretation of the Quran, the final authority of interpretation, and validity of some a*hadith*. With loss of a single broadly accepted religious authority of a caliph, and depending upon social and/or political reasons, most people started consulting and following scholar(s) of their choice. This phase continued for more than 400 years, or a little longer depending upon a particular school of thought. During this phase Islam's influence extended far beyond the Arabian Peninsula in all geographic directions. This was also the phase when large volume of primary documentational (books of *Hadiths* and *Seerah*), and interpretative (*Tavil* or *Tafsir* of the Quran) work was accomplished.

The passing of the first generations of Muslims necessitated the documentational work. The exponential growth of other intellectual work during this 3rd phase was due to the practical and juristic demands. Spread of Islam to non-Arabic speaking territories led to the "translation" of the Quran. Larger and stronger Muslim societies required a formal, written, and unified jurisprudence system to operate governmental organizations and the day-to-day peoples' business. All major religious schools of thought partly came about from these circumstances and demands. Unlike the second phase when the caliph was consulted for any clarification, in this third phase scholars assumed that role. It was important to note that, for most Muslims, this was the first time since the first revelation of the Quran that the persons consulted for final clarification in religious matters, the scholars, did not have an authoritative role in governance. This dichotomy when religious interpretation or the religious authority was separated from the business of governance, for most Muslims, continued from then on.

Muslim intellectuals not only worked in religious matters and jurisprudence, but they also helped to shape multiple other fields of study, from astronomy to biology, and mathematics to applied physics; just to name a few. This was the time, during this 3rd phase, when Muslims were at their intellectual peak. Unfortunately, though, due to the philosophical struggle within the community, and disagreement of how to cope with newly acquired knowledge, this phase ended rather abruptly around a thousand years ago. In my opinion, this phase ended with the death of the great philosopher Muhammad ibn Rushd of Andalusia around 1198. Many Muslim political dynasties continued to rule for centuries after that, but not without the loss of intellectual edge Muslims once were blessed with.

The next or the 4th phase of Muslim intellectual development has so for been the longest and continued for almost one millennium. Comparatively speaking, not as much or as significant intellectual work was accomplished in this phase as in the phase before. Muslim civilization started to crumble at the start of this phase, more in intellectual terms than political, which ultimately followed. The loss of broader intellectual exercise within the Muslim community and its introversion towards orthodoxy led to its departure from the position of intellectual and political leadership and, in fact, for most Muslim societies, loss of their freedom. This topic was beyond the scope of this treatise, but anyone interested in a little more detail may refer to a small book I co-authored with my respected friend Mirza Yawar Baig, "Muslims' Intellectual Eclipse", available on Amazon.

I am not saying that Muslims did not do intellectual work during this phase; it's that the work they did was of a different nature and significance. Examples of some exceptional intellectual work done in this phase were the work of Maulana Rumi of modern-day Turkey many centuries ago, and of Mohammad Iqbal of modern-day Pakistan many centuries later. There were other but similar examples. Aside from the nature of their work, compared to the major scholars of the previous phase, the emphasis in this phase was different. In this period of Muslim intellectual development, their work was mostly rhetorical (mastery of words and language like most poetry), usually in the form of allegorical poetry, and at times dialectical (argumentation or a dialogue with differing views). Emphasis on demonstrative work (logical analysis), which for many other civilizations opened the door for the "scientific" revolution, was limited both in theological and non-theological areas of study. The type of critical thinking and analysis required for dialectical and demonstrative work was either curtailed or just shunned. Muslims at large, and especially their intellectual elite, mostly indulged in rhetorical pastimes.

One may argue that I did not mention many scholars of this phase who were equally "significant" and provided the so-called "modern" translation of the Quran. In my opinion, if we looked closely, their work did not carry enough significance when compared to the work in the previous phase. For an Urdu speaking person, an example might be Tafheem ul Quran of Syed Abul A'ala Maudoudi. On one hand, it provided an easy-to-read Urdu translation of the Quran. But on the other, looking at it closely, the book itself and the people who claimed to be most influenced by it, never reached a higher level and could not fulfill its promise.

One significant aspect of this phase was further divergence, almost to the point of divorce, of the work of Islamic scholars from governance. For multiple reasons, scholars' loss of any direct influence upon governance, and the subsequent inability to attract and impact the community at large led to the development of alternate intellectual currents. Most famous or the most influential Muslim intellectuals of this phase, as suggested above, were not religious scholars, scientists, or the jurists, as they were in the phase before. They were the likes of Jalal ud Din Muhammad Rumi or Muhammad Iqbal, whose work was not directly about the interpretation of religious matters, or demonstrative, but rather excelling in rhetorical expression and poetic philosophy. This work with its own value and significance carried limited impact upon governance, people's practical life, or to the subject of this essay.

In my opinion, this longest phase of Muslim intellectual development ended a few years ago, not due to any direct effort by Muslims but rather by an unusual outside factor: the widespread availability of the Internet. Though there were many other factors like the personal computer, and the easy global physical accessibility, Internet changed almost every aspect of our lives, including the way religion was studied and practiced. It provided an easily accessible intellectual platform for anyone willing to access the Quran in its original text, or its various interpretations in multiple languages. Before the Internet, the Quran, the *Hadith* and the *Seerah* weren't necessarily restricted for ordinary Muslims, but for practical purposes they were not that easy to access either. With Internet, all that material, with or without human interface, was widely available for listening, reading, referencing, or researching. This present phase, the 5th phase of the Muslim intellectual development, may turn out to be their revival phase. Only Allah SWT knows best!

CHAPTER 4

WHY IS AN OPINION ALWAYS NEEDED?

During the 1st phase as described above, when the Prophet SAW was physically present, there was no issue of "difference of opinion" in religious matters within the community believing in his prophethood. He was physically there for any consultation or clarification, at times with additional guidance by the angel Jibrail, may peace be upon him! The Prophet himself was the final authority for all religious matters, especially the Quran, including its recitation and interpretation. For the faithful believers his words, opinions, and actions were final. No other opinion mattered. On the other hand, non-believers and hypocrites differed, the former overtly and the latter covertly. Aside from religion, the subject of non-religious or worldly affairs was different. There were some documented examples of such differences of opinion where the Prophet's opinion was apparently not the best one or the one accepted or implemented, in a way providing us a lesson that he was after all a human being.

In the 2nd phase, after the Prophet SAW left this world, the matter of an opinion on religious issues became different, with final authority assumed by the caliph. During this phase, at times a difference of opinion pertaining to religious and related practical matters arose within the expanding Muslim community. The difference of opinion was not about the fundamental beliefs or principles of Islam; it was mostly about their application in a rapidly expanding Muslim society. This topic of difference of opinion in early Islam was worthy of expansive discussion with multiple dimensions but was not the subject of this essay.

The difference of opinion that started in the second phase has continued to this day. Its fundamental reasons also have not changed. There are multiple reasons for which a religious opinion is and will always be needed. An outline of these reasons is as follows:

The 1st reason for an opinion: To find the exact translation or the meaning of the words of the Quran which is called *Tafsir* or *Tawil* of the Quran. There are numerous books of *Tafsir*, some small and the others expansive. *Tafsir* of the Quran is a very large subject, with its own principles, rules, and traditions. For almost any Muslim now, it is possible to access numerous books or versions of *Tafsir*. This situation is remarkably different compared to just a generation ago.

Reviewing the *Tafsir* literature in English, one may at least expect three issues:

1. Language: Early *Tafsir* work was done either in Arabic or Persian. For an English speaking or English understanding reader, access to early *Tafsir* literature

Chapter 4 – Why is an Opinion Always Needed?

is quite limited, as large part of the early work has either not been translated in English, or partly translated, or not easily available.

2. Authenticity: One may find a *Tafsir* attributed to early scholars, such as Tafsir by ibn Abbas available on the net, but its authenticity may be debatable.

3. The issue of re-translation: Some earlier work is translated in English and easily available, such as *Tafaseer ibn Kathir,* or *Tafaseer al-Qurtubi*. These *Tafseers* were originally authored in Arabic and then re-translated in English or Urdu. Because of limitations of difference in linguistic vocabulary, re-translated work always carried higher chance of misunderstandings.

Other than these issues, one shall also be careful about write-ups, which are purposefully deviant, and designed to misguide readers. Internet is not deficient of this type of propaganda material.

I consulted following volumes of *Tafaseer* for this treatise. First three in the list are re-translation from original Arabic version. Many are authored in English language, while some are in Urdu:

1. Tafsir al-Qurtubi by Abu Abdullah Al-Qurtubi (1214-1273)

2. Tafsir Ibn Kathir by Abu al-Fida Umar ibn Kathir (1300-1373)

3. Tafsir al-Jalalayn by Jalal ad-Din al-Mhalli and Jalal ad-Din as-Suyuti (1459, 1505)

4. The Meaning of the Holy Quran by Abdullah Yusuf Ali (1872-1953)

5. The Glorious Quran by Muhammad Marmaduke Pickthall (1875-1936)

6. Tafhim ul Quran by Abul A'la Maududi (1903-1979)

7. Tadabbur-i-Quran by Amin Ahsan Ilahi (1904-1997)

8. The Noble Quran by Dr. Muhammad Taqi-ud-Din Al-Hilali, PH.D. & Dr. Muhammad Muhsin Khan (published in 2011)

9. *Tafsir* by Allama Hussain Baksh (published in 1993)

10. The Gracious Quran by Ahmad Zaki Hammad (published in 2008)

11. Al-Quran ul Karim, Translation and *Tafsir* sponsored by Saudi Arabian government.

12. Quran Hakim, by Maulana Sayyed Shabbir Ahmad, (published in 2004)

13. Meaning of the Noble Quran, by Muhammad Taqi Usmani (1943)

14. The Study Quran edited by Seyyed Hossein Nasr (published in 2015)

15. The Clear Quran, by Dr. Mustafa Khattab, 2016.

Going through the *Tafsir* literature one may find a variety of opinions, both within early and later generations of

Muslim scholars. Other than difference of opinion about interpretation of an *ayah*, one can also not overlook the fact that sometimes opinions are less than satisfactory, some in fact tenuous. The reader shall be particularly careful, or at least be aware that, while reading the Quran translation, the word(s) or wording within parenthesis, the annotations, are added by the translator(s). Its intended purpose probably is clarification for an average reader as in the first example underneath, but many times it is more like a particular ideological slant, as in the second one:

The Quran, Al-Ikhlas, *ayah* 1 (Al-Quran 112:1)

> "Say: He is Allah the One and Only;" Ali.
> "Say (O Muhammd [SAW]): "He is Allah, (the) One." Al-Hilali & Khan.

The Quran, Al-Fatiha, *ayah* 7 (Al-Quran 1:7)
> "The way of those on whom Thou hast bestowed Thy Grace, those whose (portion) is not wrath and who go not astray." Ali

> "The Way of those on whom You have bestowed Your Grace, not (the way) of those who earned Your Anger (such as the Jews), nor of those who went astray (such as the Christians)." Al-Hilali & Khan.

In the example above, accepting or preferring one translation over the other significantly alters the implications and significance of the underlying message. It leads to a rather "restrictive" understanding of the underlying message of the *ayah*, which is not an uncommon problem with some translations with excessive annotations.

In addition, it is a reasonably well-accepted concept that the *ayat* of the Quran carry multiple layers or shades of meaning and significance. If that is the case, annotations significantly restrict the reader to a particular opinion. For a discerning reader, it is best to find a translation without any or minimal inserted comments, but at the same time spending every effort to go through all different opinions about an *ayah*. In this context, I again find Abdullah Yusuf Ali's translation better than many others.

The 2nd reason for an opinion: To find the authenticity, meaning, and significance of a *hadith* or a part of the *Seerah* of the Prophet SAW. The *Hadith* literature is also diverse, much more than the *Tafseer* of the Quran. The diversity in *hadith* literature indirectly reflected the amount of difference of opinion on this subject.

Unlike translation of the Quran where numerous options (translations done by different scholars) are available, the *Hadith* translation is quite limited. In most cases, the available translated version is seldom more than one. Sometimes one may find about a translation, but it may not be available for purchase. For example, I reviewed two translations of the Sahih al Bukhari, one by M. Muhsin Khan and the other by Hilal Yayinlari. Other than linguistic differences in the translation of same *ahadith*, one may also find a significant variance between the contents of these two books. I find this issue particularly disturbing because the primary purpose of books of *Hadith* was documentation, not opinion or jurisprudence. But, despite easy accessibility of printing and digitization, one may find that the newer versions of these sacred books, for whatever reason are abridged. It is a terribly short-sighted idea, as none of us has any right to miss even a single word of a book of *Hadith* while we try to translate these precious and sacred texts. I hope the Muslim community in the West may undertake this project and faithfully translate these critically important books in their original design and content.

Finally, one shall always be mindful of the critical difference between the Quran and the *Hadith*, the former being the revealed words of Allah SWT, and the latter, a documentation of historical accounts, as remembered by the people witnessing them, mostly recorded decades, or generations after they took place.

Following is a list of the major books of the *Hadith:*

1. **Al-Muwatta**
   By Malik bin Anas (93AH to 179AH, Madinah)

2. **Musnad**
   By Ahmad bin Hanbal (164AH to 241AH, Baghdad)

3. **Sahih al Bukhari**
   By Muhammad al-Bukhari (194AH to 256AH, Uzbekistan)

4. **Sahih Muslim**
   By Muslim ibn al-Hajjaj (199 AH to 261 AH, Persia)

5. **Sunan Abu Dawood**
   By Sulayman Abu Dawood (202 AH to 275AH, Persia)

6. **Sunan at-Tirmidhi**
   By Muhammad at-Tirmidhi (209 AH to 279AH, Uzbekistan)

7. Al-Sunan al Sughra
By Ahmad Al-Nasai (214 AH to 303AH, Persia)

8. Sunan ibn Majah
By Muhammad ibn Majah (208 AH to 273AH, Persia)

9. Kitab al-Kafi
By Muhammad al-Kulayni (250AH to 329 AH, Iran/Iraq)

10. Man la yahduruhu al-Faqih
By Muhammad al-Qummi (310 AH to 380 AH, Persia)

11. Tahdhib al-Ahkam
By Muhammad Hasan Tusi (384 AH to 459, Persia)

12. Al-Istibsar
By Muhammad Hasan Tusi (384AH to 459AH, Persia)

The books on *Seerah* (mainly based upon the *Hadith*) Many

The 3rd reason for an opinion: To find answer to a question not directly or explicitly addressed in the Quran, the *Hadith* or the *Seerah*

Chapter 5

Interpretation or Translation of the Quran

The Quran is a book unlike any other humans ever experienced before or after its revelation. It is with only one version and one edition, though minor linguistic or spelling variations, without altering the meaning or the message, do exist. It is not like a typical textbook where topics are classified or categorized. More than 14 centuries have passed and no one has ever found any mistake or a flaw or falsehood in this book. Not comprehending or accepting or believing in its message is a different matter. It was revealed in a somewhat piecemeal fashion based mostly upon circumstances around the life of the Prophet Muhammad SAW and the new Muslim community over a period of 23 years. Later it was compiled in the format known to us, with 114 *surahs*. Its compilation and the order of *surahs* was due to some divine reasoning and was not based upon the order of revelation, the size of *surahs*, or some other discernable pattern. The Prophet Muhammad SAW, guided by the angel Jibrail AS, himself accomplished this fundamental task.

Like any other language, in today's world, one may identify multiple Arabic dialects with different levels of variations in pronunciation, delivery, and grammar. The language of the Quran, sometimes described as the Classical Arabic, is not spoken by majority of contemporary Arabic speakers. It is incorrect to assume that any Arabic speaking person may fully or easily grasp the Quranic Arabic. Of course, not every English-speaking person understands the Shakespearian English. Quranic Arabic is the ultimate form of literary Arabic, with its rhetorical beauty and sagacious depth. Even then, part of the language of the Quran seems simple and relatively easy to understand, while another large part is quite poetic, in fact a literary masterpiece, neither completely in prose and nor in poetry.

The first and the initial generations of Muslims spoke and understood the Quranic Arabic. This was the language of the Quraysh tribe of Arabia, the tribe the Prophet SAW belonged to. As Islam spread to the larger Arabian Peninsula and especially to the non-Arabic speaking areas, a need arose to describe the meaning and interpretation of the words of the Quran. According to the Google search today, the Quran has been translated in part in 114, and in full in 47 languages. Ability to understand the Quranic language, or its translation, does not guarantee that one may really fathom the message an *ayah* is delivering, but it is the first essential step. Of note, despite their command of the Classical Arabic, there are many *ayat* of the Quran whose meaning was almost certainly not known to the first generation of Muslims and became clear many centuries later.

Chapter 5 – Interpretation or Translation of the Quran

The subject matter of the Quran is diverse, which I try to outline a little later. It is a book not just for a certain generation, a particular time-period, or a specific population. It is a book for everyone for all the times. It is a guide for both, someone with an average or anyone with an exceptional intellect. It is a guide for anyone, or everyone provided they comprehend and believe in Allah SWT's true position, as, for example, described in the Quran (*Ayat ul Kursi*), and the status of His last Prophet Muhammad SAW:

The Quran, Al-Baqarah, *ayah* 255 (Al-Quran 2:255)

"Allah! There is no god but He – the Living, the Selfsubsisting, Eternal. No slumber can seize Him nor sleep. His are all things in the heavens and on earth. Who is there that can intercede in His presence except as He permitteth? He knoweth what (appearth to His creatures as) Before or After or Behind them. Nor shall they compass aught of His Knowledge except as He willeth. His Throne doth extend over the heavens and the earth, and He feeleth no fatigue in guarding and preserving them for He is the Most High, the Supreme (in glory)." Ali.

"Allah! *La ilaha illa Huwa* (none has the right to be worshipped but He), the Ever Living, the One Who sustains and protects all that exists. Neither slumber, nor sleep overtakes Him. To Him belongs whatever is in the heavens and whatever is on earth. Who is he that can intercede with Him except with His Permission? He knows what happens to them (His creatures) in this world, and what will happen to them in the Hereafter. And they will never compass anything of His Knowledge except that which He wills. His *Kursi* extends over the heavens and the earth, and He feels no fatigue in guarding and preserving them. And He is the Most High, the Most Great." Al-Hilali & Khan.

The Quran, Al-Ahzab, *ayah* 40 (Al-Quran 33:40)

> "Muhammad is not the father of any of your men, but (he is) the Messenger of Allah, and the Seal of the Prophets. And Allah has full knowledge of all things." Ali.

> "Muhammad (SAW) is not the father of any man among you, but he is the Messenger of Allah and the last (end) of the Prophets. And Allah is Ever All-Aware of everything." Al-Hilali & Khan.

For many, the message of the Quranic words is simple and straightforward. For others, it carries multiple layers or shades of meaning, many hitherto unknown. On one side, the Quran covers numerous aspects of human life, while on the other, many scientific facts and secrets of this universe. It mentions many historical events, though it is not a book of history. Its words and sentences with their order and reiterations, like tones and melodies of a delightful symphony, intertwined but also distinct, are a source of solace for a believing listener, and intellectual challenge for a discernable elite. One may also compare it to a huge sea of knowledge, knowledge that is mostly hidden under its waves, even to the ones navigating through its expanse.

All believers, if they try, with or without a specific requirement of a guide, are free to navigate and enjoy its bounties. The basic unit of the Quran is an *ayah* (a sign), as each of the *ayat* (plural of *ayah*) represent a sign from Allah SWT. Most readers of the Quran do not speak Arabic, and most Arabic speaking people do not use the Quranic Arabic in their common speech. It is a common observation that most people who read the Quran only surf it and stay at its surface, mostly reciting and enjoying its rhetorical rhythm and colloquial beauty. A minority tries to understand the meaning of its words. Many complain about the abundance of its repetitive messages, like complaining about the salt in the seawater, ignoring its logic. Few are really blessed: With a proper intention and the will, a sustained effort, sometimes with additional help of a guide, and even more importantly through the divine guidance bestowed upon them, they can navigate its expanse, and appreciate some of its hidden treasures.

One way to understand the Quran is to divide its *ayat* based upon subject matter, as I have tried in the following:

Foundational: These *ayat* address fundamental aspects of Islam, e.g., the concept of *Taoheed*, the Unseen, the Afterlife, the Garden (*Jannah*) and the Fire (*Jahannam*). They also elaborate attributes of Allah SWT, and His creations.

Parables: Many messages in the Quran are conveyed in parables.
Historical: It is by no means a book of history, but the Quran includes many historical references especially related to some of the previous prophets of Allah SWT.

Reminders: For example, repeated messages for *taoheed*, praying, fasting, and charity.

Rules and Regulations: These *ayat* cover details of what is allowed and/or prohibited.

Scientific and Miraculous: Numerous *ayat* providing information that we typically consider scientific, some already proven and many still unexplained.

Supplications: They are spread across the Quran, from the first page to the last.

Miscellaneous: This also included *ayat* with a single or just a few letters without making a formal word, whose meaning so far is unknown.

The Concept of Abrogation:

It is important to comment briefly about the concept of "abrogation". It is clearly mentioned in the Quran that if an *ayah* was abrogated, a better was brought in its place. But there is no specific mention in the Quran that an abrogated *ayah* is part of the Quran. There is no authentic *hadith* or narration of the Prophet SAW where he might have discussed the issue of abrogated *ayat* in the Quran or specified them. This concept evolved later likely due to the juristic demands, and analysis of multiple *ayat* addressing the same subject. For those who might get offended with what I just stated, they should know that it was not uncommon to find difference of opinion about this subject even within early generation well-respected scholars. This issue is one of the reasons for difference of religious opinion within the larger Muslim community.

Scholars in the past have described multiple types or levels of abrogation. The first one was when the Quran explicitly provided evidence for abrogation of a previously provided instruction or information. Usually quoted example was the *ayat* about change in the direction of *Qiblah*.

The Quran Al-Baqarah, *ayat* 143-144 (Al-Quran 2:143-144)

> "Thus have We made of you an *Ummah* justly balanced, that ye might be witnesses over the nations, and the Messenger a witness over yourselves; and We appointed the *Qiblah* to which thou wast used, only to test those who followed the Messenger from those who would turn on their heels (From the Faith). Indeed it was (a change) momentous, except to those guided by Allah. And never would Allah make your faith of no effect. For Allah is to all people most surely full of kindness, Most Merciful. We see the turning of thy face (for guidance) to the heavens; now shall We turn thee to a *Qiblah* that shall please thee. Turn then thy face in the direction of the Sacred Mosque: wherever ye are, turn your faces in that direction. The people of the Book know well that that is the truth from their Lord nor is Allah unmindful of what they do." Ali.

> "Thus We have made you [true Muslims – real believers of Islamic Monotheism, true followers of Prophet Muhammad SAW and his Sunnah (legal ways)], a *Wasat* (just) (and the best) nation, that you be witnesses over mankind and the Messenger (Muhammad SAW) be a witness over you. And We made the *Qiblah* (prayer direction towards Jerusalem) which you used to face, only to test those who followed the Messenger (Muhammad SAW) from those who would turn on their heels (i.e., disobey the Messenger). Indeed it was great (heavy) except for those whom Allah guided. And Allah would never

make your faith (prayers) to be lost (i.e., your prayers offered towards Jerusalem). Truly, Allah is full of kindness, the Most Merciful towards mankind. Verily! We have seen the turning of your (Muhammad's SAW) face towards the heaven. Surely, We shall turn you to a *Qiblah* (prayer direction) that shall please you, so turn your face in the direction of Al-Masjid- al-Haram (at Makkah). And wheresoever you people are, turn your faces (in prayer) in that direction. Certainly, the people who were given the Scriptures (i.e., Jews and the Christians) know well that, that (your turning towards the direction of the Ka'bah at Makkah in prayers) is the truth from their Lord. And Allah is not unaware of what they do." Al-Hilali & Khan.

The Quran, Al-Baqarah, *ayah* 149 (Al-Quran 2: 149)

"From whencesoever thou startest forth turn thy face in the direction of the Sacred Mosque; that is indeed the truth from thy Lord. And Allah is not unmindful of what ye do." Ali.

"And from wheresoever you start forth (for prayers), turn your face in the direction of Al-Masjid-AlHaram (at Makkah), that is indeed the truth from your Lord. And Allah is not unaware of what you do." Al-Hilali & Khan.

These *ayat* provide explicit instructions of change in the direction of *Qiblah* from one sacred mosque (in Jerusalem) to the other (in Makkah). But it does not mean that any of these *ayat* was abrogated, they are still part of the Quran with their full meaning. The message

Chapter 5 – Interpretation or Translation of the Quran

these *ayat* conveyed is also all- valid. It is not an example of an abrogated *ayah*, but rather an abrogation of a practice, or the Sunnah. Muslims, as instructed by the Prophet SAW, prayed facing the sacred mosque in Jerusalem until these *ayat* were revealed, and the direction of the *Qiblah* was changed. These *ayat* also provide an example of the supreme status of the Quran and the instructions within, as I outlined above while describing intellectual underpinning of Islam.

Another commonly used example for abrogation is following, about alcohol drinking, which, like *Riba,* was permissible in early Islam until it was outlawed:

The Quran, Al-Nahl, ayah 67 (Al-Quran 16:67):

> "And from the fruit of the date-palm and the vine, ye get out wholesome drink, and food: behold in this also is a Sign for those who are wise." Ali.
> "And from the fruits of date-palms and grapes, you derive strong drink (this was before the order of the prohibition of the alcoholic drinks) and a goodly provision. Verily, therein is indeed a sign for people who have wisdom." Al-Hilali & Khan.

The Quran, Al-Baqarh, *ayah* 219 (Al-Quran 2:219)

> "They ask thee concerning wine and gambling. Say: "In them is great sin, and some profit, for men; but the sin is greater than the profit . . . .". Ali.

> "They ask you (O Muhammad SAW) concerning alcoholic drink and gambling. Say: "In them is

a great sin, and (some) benefit, for men, but the sin of them is greater than their benefit . . . ". Al-Hilali & Khan.

Al Quran, Al-Nisa, *ayah* 43 (Al-Quran 4:43)

"O ye who believe! Approach not prayers with a mind befogged, until ye can understand all that ye say- . . . ". Ali.

"O you who believe! Approach not As-Salat (the prayer) when you are in a drunken state until you know (the meaning) of what you utter...". Al-Hilali & Khan.

Al Quran, Al-Maidah, *ayah* 90-91 (Al-Quran 5:90-91)

"O ye who believe! Intoxicants and gambling, (dedication of) stones, and (divination by) arrows, are an abomination- of Satan's handiwork; eschew such (abomination), that ye may prosper. Satan's plan is (but) to excite enmity and hatred between you, with intoxicants and gambling, and hinder you from the remembrance of Allah, and from prayer: will ye not then abstain?" Ali

"O you who believe! Intoxicants (all kinds of alcoholic drinks), gambling, *Al-Ansab* , and *Al-Azlam* (arrows for seeking luck or decision) are an abomination of *Shaitan*'s (Satan) handiwork. So avoid (strictly all) that (abomination) in order that you may be successful. *Shaitan* (Satan) wants only to excite enmity and hatred between you with intoxicants (alcoholic drinks) and gambling, and hinder you from the remembrance of Allah and from *As-Salat* (the prayer). So, will you not then abstain?" Al-Hilali & Khan.

Despite different shades or levels of prohibitions against intoxicants (such as alcohol), none of these *ayat* recommend alcohol drinking. For example, the first *ayah* in the list is talking about what people did and not what people should do. Also, it mentions "wholesome" or "strong" drinks but not specifically an intoxicant. The reference was to some drinks, the example of which could be the grape juice, or a non-intoxicating drink made from dates, which, as per the *Hadith*, the Prophet SAW used to enjoy. Messages of these *ayat*, which seem to vary, are not mutually exclusive. The wisdom of inclusion of these *ayat* within the Quran with different shades of meaning, and there are many such examples, is an altogether different subject. A subject that is also interesting and rather large but not the topic of this work.

Is meaning of every *ayah* of the Quran known to us?

The first step towards knowing the meaning of the Quran requires understanding every word of an *ayah*, or its meaning, the so-called word-by-word translation. The next step is to figure out multiple layers of meaning an *ayah* may convey. As stated above, during the initial phase of the Quranic revelation, the Prophet SAW was the final arbiter of the Quran. In his lifetime, through his speeches and statements, he provided explanation or clarifications (i.e., *Tafsir* or *Tavil*) of the Quranic *ayat*. Unfortunately, though, there was very limited documentation about this subject, and because of this deficiency most *ayat* of the Quran are open to interpretation, which has resulted in variance of opinion. In general, *Tafseer* by earlier Muslim generations is respected more than others, but it does not mean that they had full understanding of every *ayah* of the Quran. For example, let's look at the following *ayah,* whose real meaning and significance became known to humans, centuries later:

Al Quran, Al-Anbiya, *ayah* 30 (Al-Quran 21:30)

> "Do not the unbelievers see that the heavens and the earth were joined together (as one unit of Creation), before We clove them asunder? We made from water every living thing. Will they not then believe?" Ali.

> "Have not those who disbelieve known that the heavens and the earth were joined together as one united piece, then We parted them? And We have made from water every living thing. Will they not then believe?" Al-Hilali & Khan.

Like the above *ayah* whose meaning and significance was not understood for centuries, the real meaning and significance of the following *ayah* is still not known and open to interpretation:

Al Quran, Adh-Dhariyat, *ayah* 7 (Al-Quran 51:7)

> "By the Sky with (its) numerous Paths," Ali.

> "By the heaven full of paths," Al-Hilali & Khan.

CHAPTER 6

THE HADITH – OF THE PROPHET SAW

The mere fact that there are multiple books of *Hadith* with significant differences in content is a reflection upon not just the difference of opinion but also its causes. The science of *Hadith* by itself is a complex and intricate subject, including how a*hadith* were initially documented, and later collected and scrutinized, and then cataloged. It is generally understood that the process of documentation of *Hadith* started when the Prophet SAW was alive. I am not aware of any physical evidence available today for confirmation. In any case, further formal steps leading to its compilation and cataloging in a book format were taken about a century later. A general understanding of this process, the so-called science of *Hadith*, is helpful for a reader to understand and appreciate the variety in *Hadith* literature. It may also help to avoid unnecessary confusion from a cursory reading, especially for a believer.

In general, Muslims accepted a *hadith* valid if its origin was found to be valid, through documentation or through reliable narrators. One major difference of opinion, for one reason or the other, was about the acceptance or rejection of a narrator of a *hadith*, or his or her reliability. This impacted validity of a *hadith* directly in case of a single or the first narrator, or indirectly in a chain of narrators. As one might expect, at times there also was difference of opinion about the content of a *hadith*. In some situations, difference of opinion existed about the meaning of what was stated by the Prophet SAW.

Scholars tried to deal with the issue of authenticity by categorizing a*hadith* in terms of level of authenticity. This classification system was developed more than 100-300 years after Prophet's passing, depending upon the author. All acceptable *ahadith* were generally divided in three categories: *sahih*, *hasan*, and *daeef*, which can be translated as sound, good, and weak, based upon the level of available evidence. This may not be the place to discuss details of this classification, but one must accept that the *hadith* literature is not like the Quran and is based upon varying degrees of authenticity. This issue is one of the critical reasons for difference of opinion within Islamic thought process, resulting in evolution of different schools of thought, while also contributing to the sectarian differences.

In my opinion, all this is nothing unusual for a topic as complex as documenting biography (*Seerah*) and oral statements of a person as significant and prolific as the Prophet Muhammad SAW. In fact, looking at it in a different way, there is no other example in human history where so much is documented and/or known about a human being as the Prophet Muhammad SAW, both about his public and private life. A reasonable and discernible reader may easily *read through* any "questionable" or confusing account in the *Hadith* and the *Seerah*. It is impossible to ignore the overwhelming amount of information available to us about the Prophet SAW as a person, and what he represented, except maybe by someone peeking through biased lenses. A dirty lens can never clarify a perspective even if the view is clear and eyes are not diseased.

Despite differences, one may find in different books of *Hadith*, including the differences in translations, one cannot over-emphasize its religious significance. Almost all Islamic practices, including Islamic finance, cannot be completely understood, and practiced without guidance from the *Hadith*. The Prophet SAW's life, available to us in the form of his biography and the *Hadith*, is a user's manual without which the practice of Islam is neither recommended nor conceivable.

What shall one do then? How shall one handle these differences? The key to that process is the understanding of the fundamental underlying principles of Islam. Foremost of that is the understanding of the Quran, and the value of the *Hadith* as alluded to in the previous paragraph. In addition, what is needed is an open mind and heart to analyze what one may have previously understood about a *hadith* or a subject like Islamic finance. One must also be willing to revisit an understanding of a subject matter to see if the Quran and/or the *Hadith* supported it, or if it is consistent with the fundamental principles of Islam. And if that is not the case, it may have been incorrect. In that case, I recommend further reading, researching, reflecting, seeking help if needed, and at any cost continuing the intellectual struggle until the right satisfactory answer is found. Unfortunately, most people do not go through this process, and of those who do, most falter and avoid the challenge of self- analysis and correction.

Discrepancy in the *Hadith* Literature

The *Hadith* is the description of historical events, reported by people witnessing a conversation, or an occurrence related to the life of Prophet Muhammad SAW. There could be more than one reason for difference of opinion, such as memory of the original and especially the subsequent narrators, context, mode of expression (which could change the underlying message), misunderstandings, willfully discounting some narrators, or just plain wrong intention resulting in falsification. Early *Hadith* scholars painstakingly considered these or any other related issues, and collected and cataloged a*hadith*, which, as per their research and as much as possible, were free of falsehood. Despite that, to say that all these matters were completely settled and resolved is an indefensible statement. It is a sensitive topic to address, usually making people particularly upset, and defensive. Anyone who tries to critique this matter may easily be labeled as *"Hadith* denier," and is frequently castigated. In my opinion, ignoring this subject has not only resulted in more problems and divisions within the Muslim community, but it also takes people away from the message and the spirit of Islam.

The first formal compilation of *Hadith* that I could find was the Al-Muwatta of Imam Malik ibn Anas of Madinah, may Allah SWT be pleased with him. This was probably compiled about 120 years after Prophet SAW passed away. *Ahadith* were just a part of this relatively small book. It also carried opinions of the Imam and the

Chapter 6 – The Hadith – of the Prophet SAW

people of Madinah of that time-period. All other books of *Hadith* available to us and listed above were compiled later, during a 50–350year time-period. Translation of the *Hadith* to English or other languages was done only recently and resulted in additional potential source of confusion and error.

The *Hadith* literature is very large, and most of it is without any contradiction or overt confusion. There are more a*hadith* in Sahih Al-Bukhari (about 7,563) than *ayat* of the Quran (6,236), and that is just one of the many versions of books of *Hadith*. In comparison to that, there are more than 27,000 *ahadith* in the Musnad of Imam ibn Hanbal! Probably, the largest issue about the *Hadith* is what is preferred by the so-called 'Shias', versus 'Sunnis', though the Prophet and his associates never made any such distinction. The *Hadith* literature, most of it, is not revealed knowledge, but rather a documentation of peoples' reporting about their interactions with the Prophet SAW, or his associates. Due to the pivotal nature of *Hadith* in Islamic practices and jurisprudence, any discrepancy in *Hadith* literature, its translation or interpretation, cannot be ignored, and shall be dealt with intelligently and logically. Resolving such issues may very well help us improve our understanding of the Prophet SAW, the Quran, and Islam. Following is just an example of this issue:

> Sahih Al-Bukhari2, Vol 3, XXXIV, Chapter 26, 299: Narrated Aun bin Abu Juhaifa: My father bought a slave who practiced the profession of cupping. (My father broke the slave's instrument of cupping). I asked my father why he had done so? He replied, "The Prophet SAW forbade the acceptance of the price of a dog or blood, and

also forbade the profession of tattooing, getting tattooed and accepting or give *Riba* (usury) and cursed the picture-makers."

Sahih Al-Bukhari3 Vol 3, Chapter 34, 2086. Narrated Aun bin Abu Juhaifa: My father bought a slave who practiced the profession of cupping. (My father broke the slave's instruments of cupping). I asked my father why he had done so. He replied, "The Prophet SAW forbade the acceptance of the price of a dog or blood, and also forbade the profession of tattooing, or getting tattooed and the eater of Riba (usury), and also the one who gives it, and cursed the picture makers."

Sunan Abu Dawud Vol. 4, Chapter 38, 3421. It was narrated from Rafi bin Khadij that the Messenger of Allah SAW said: "The earnings of a cupper are impure (*Khabith*), the price of a dog is impure and the earning of a *Baghi* (prostitute) is impure." (Sahih)

Sahih Al-Bukhari3 Vol. 3, Chapter 34, 2102: Narrated Anas bin Malik RA: Abu Taiba cupped Allah's Messenger SAW. So he SAW ordered that he be paid one Sa of dates and ordered his masters to reduce his tax (as he was a slave and had to pay tax to them).

Sahih Al-Bukhari3 Vol. 3, Chapter 34, 2103:

Narrated Ibn Abbas RA: Once the Prophet SAW got his blood out (medically) and paid that person who had done it. If it had been illegal, the Prophet SAW would not have paid him.

Sahih Muslim Vol 4, 22, Chapter 11, [4038] 62 – (1577). It was narrated that Humaid said: "Anas bin Malik was asked about the earnings of a cupper and he said: 'The Messenger of Allah was treated with cupping by Abu Taibah, and he ordered that he be given two Sa of food. He spoke to his masters, and they waived their portion of his earnings, and he said: 'The best thing with which you may be treated is cupping,' or 'it is one of the best of your remedies.'"

Sunan Ibn Majah, Vol. 3, The Chapter on Business Transactions, Chapter 10, 2165: It was narrated that Abu Mas'ud, 'Uqbah bin 'Amr said: "The Messenger of Allah SAW forbade the earnings of a cupper." (Sahih)

These *ahadith* provide examples of contradictory statements. One may take a position that one or some of these a*hadith* about cupping, based upon integrity of narrators, is more accurate than others, but that is a different and expansive subject. My point is that in some situations, within the *Hadith* literature available to us, there is disagreement.

It may be important to note that the matter of paying for cupping, a practice mostly abolished at this time, may seem a trivial subject to discuss, but it is of tremendous significance. In a way, in an Islamic society, it provides the religious basis for a physician or a surgeon to be able to charge for the service rendered.

Following is another example of apparent contradiction:

Sunan Abu Dawud, Vol. 4, 3348. It was narrated that 'Umar said: "The Messenger of Allah SAW said: 'Gold for silver is *Riba* unless exchanged on the spot; wheat for wheat is *Riba* unless exchanged on the spot; **dates for dates is *Ribã* unless exchanged on the spot**; and barley for barley is *Riba*, unless exchanged on the spot."

Sahih Al-Bukhari2. Vol 3, Chapter 35, 506. Narrated Abu Said al-Khudri RA: Once Bilal RA brought Barni (ie, a kind of dates) to the Prophet SAW and the Prophet asked him, "From where have you brought these?" Bilal replied, "I had some inferior type of dates and exchanged two Sa's of it for one Sa of Barni dates in order to give it to the Prophet to eat." Thereupon the Prophet said, " Beware! Beware! This is definitely *Riba* (usury)! This is definitely *Riba* (usury)! Don't do so, but if you want to buy (a superior kind of dates) sell the inferior dates for money and then buy the superior kind of dates with that money."

Reading the above *hadith* from Sunan abu Dawn, the message is that bartering dates for dates is *Riba* unless it is done hand-to-hand or on the spot, but the next *hadith* is telling us that bartering of dates for dates done on the spot or hand-to-hand can still be *Riba*. As far as the first *hadith* is concerned, further explanation or the qualifying statement is missing, without which a part of it seems to be contradicting the second *hadith*. These examples in the *Hadith* literature bring us to an important and intellectually technical subject seldom mentioned or discussed within religious discourse, the subject of **internal consistency**, which I discuss in the next chapter.

The reader may note that I am using the term '*Hadith* literature', which is intentional. Every *Hadith* available to us today, in every book of the *Hadith*, is someone's description of an event, sometimes recorded and documented decades after the event took place. There is no single standard, like the Quran, where a scholar or a reader can go and check a *hadith's* validity other than going through different similar books, which taken altogether is referred to as the *Hadith* literature.

CHAPTER 7

THE CONCEPT OF INTERNAL CONSISTENCY

Internal consistency is a hallmark of successful systems. Systems do not operate well until every part of the system follow the desired rules and regulations. With something not in sync, it may run for a while or sputter along but at some point, it will falter or fail, and may never fulfill its intended goal. This is true for a machine, our own body, an institution like a company, and for a philosophical or religious doctrine. When a case of an influential person with charge of stealing was brought to the Prophet SAW, and some people tried to intervene asking for leniency because of his/her social position, the Prophet SAW was visibly upset. He famously stated that (paraphrasing) his decision would not change even if this were his own daughter instead of this person. For any system to work, internal consistency is a fundamental requirement.

Similar but an even clearer and stronger message is in the Quran:

The Quran, Al-Nisa, *ayah* 135, (Al-Quran 4:135).

> "O ye who believe! Stand out firmly for justice, as witnesses to Allah, even as against yourselves, or your parents, or your kin, and whether it be (against) rich or poor: For Allah can best protect both. Follow not the lusts (of your hearts), lest ye swerve, and if ye distort (justice) or decline to do justice, verily Allah is well-acquainted with all that ye do." Ali.

> "O you who believe! Stand out firmly for justice, as witnesses to Allah, even though it be against yourselves, or your parents, or your kin, be he rich or poor, Allah is a Better Protector to both (than you). So follow not the lusts (of your hearts), lest you may avoid justice, and if you distort your witness or refuse to give it, verily, Allah is Ever Well-Acquainted with what you do." Al-Hilali & Khan.

The Quran itself, provides the significance and justification of the concept of internal consistency:

The Quran, Al-Nisa *ayah* 82 (Al-Quran 4:82):

> "Do they not consider the Quran (with care)? Had it been from other than Allah, they would surely have found therein much discrepancy." Ali.

> "Do they not then consider the Qur'an carefully? Had it been from other than Allah, they would surely have found therein much contradictions." Al-Hilal & Khan.

Chapter 7– The Concept of Internal Consistency

There is a well-known American legal concept that one may not have to speak or testify against oneself or his/ her own interests, to avoid self-incrimination; the so-called, "taking the Fifth." The Islamic concept of conduct and justice does not include any such notion. As per Islamic principle elaborated above in the Quran, one may not withhold testimony even if it incriminates his or her own self, relatives, or other interests. Doing it is internally inconsistent with the message of Islam, especially in a situation that may result in damage to a party or a cause, which may lead to numerous socio-political problems. Unfortunately, examples of such behavior in Islamic societies are rampant, resulting in numerous discords and injustices, both at the family and societal level.

Manufacturers and companies spend a lot of energy and effort to maintain systemic consistency, or they try their best to remove any systemic inconsistencies. If the Constitution of a country states that "All men are created equal," or "All men are equal in a court of law," any regulation or practice conflicting with this notion may result in systematic and systemic failure. The country's rules, regulations, and practices must be consistent with the principles outlined in the Constitution. In this manner, Islam is not an exception. When the Prophet SAW in his famous sermon at Arafat stated, "(paraphrasing) no Arab or white has superiority over a non-Arab or black", he did not make any exceptions of the kind like the family, clan, position, or wealth, except one, the righteousness, or God-consciousness.

For our benefit, Allah SWT promised to protect the Principle of Islam, or the Quran, in its original format. Its purpose is to provide guidance to human beings to navigate through this life in a manner prescribed by its author, Allah SWT, the All-Wise. The Prophet Muhammad SAW was the channel bringing the Quran to this world.

During his 23 years of later life, the Prophet SAW provided the model of a life based upon the Quranic principles. In addition, he provided opinions in multiple fashions that addressed a wide variety of issues. Islam came to us in a full package, the principles, and a detailed manual. Unlike the Quran though, there is the matter of difference of opinion regarding the *Hadith* and the *Seerah* of the Prophet, of which we shall be aware of, acknowledge it, be truthful about it, and accordingly deal with it.

In addition, we should also be cognizant of either ill intention or ignorance. For example, let's review the following *hadith*:

> Sahih Bukhari[2], Vol. 3, XXXI, Chapter 13, 137: Narrated by Ibn Umar RA: The Prophet SAW said, "We are an illiterate nation; we neither write, nor know accounts. The month is like this and this, i.e., sometimes 29 days and sometimes of thirty days."

It is difficult to figure out exactly what was that Prophet was referring to. He was probably making a comment about peoples' general intellectual status and related practices of his time. Some may take the first part of the *hadith* separately without context, or some may accept this statement as an instruction instead of an observation of the Prophet. But it is difficult to accept it that way, as it results in an internal inconsistency between

Chapter 7– The Concept of Internal Consistency

the message of the Quran and the *hadith,* as there are clear directions in the Quran, according to which gaining knowledge and writing of financial contracts is made compulsory. Statement of the Prophet SAW in this *hadith* must be understood with proper perspective, time, and the situation to avoid any misunderstanding or internal inconsistency. When trying to understand or explain a subject matter as complex and multi-dimensional as finance, it is important to make sure that our understandings and explanations are internally consistent with the larger Islamic principles.

Without internal consistency, any system, including a religious or a philosophical doctrine, can stumble. For example, an understanding of what is understood from a *hadith* cannot be inconsistent with what is stated in the Quran; otherwise, it will become internally inconsistent. So, whatever one may understand from a *hadith* has to be consistent with what is stated in the Quran, thus making that understanding internally consistent. Interestingly, one may be tempted to make the reverse argument that any understanding we may have from the Quran has to be consistent with the *Hadith*, as the Prophet SAW spent his life based upon the Quran. Though theoretically attractive, in my opinion, because of its nature and the differences in the *Hadith* literature available to us, in many situations, it is best to forgo this un-winnable argument.

CHAPTER 8

FORMAL DIFFERENCE OF OPINION IN ISLAM – MAJOR ISLAMIC SCHOOLS OF THOUGHT

As stated above, during the 3rd or what I describe as the formative phase of Islam's intellectual development, the larger Muslim community lost the larger consensus it previously held, both in political and religious matters. First, the most significant difference with its roots in socio-political issues divided the *Ummah* in the so-called *Shia* and the *Sunni* factions. Their scholars, by reasoning and justifications from the same book, the Quran, and the life of the same prophet, Muhammad SAW, formulated their arguments with a variety of overtones, and further sub-divided each one of them. Muslim society became exponentially large and equally diverse, a typical milieu for differences of opinion. Following is the list of better-known schools of thought with their intellectual head, and timeline of origin.

The Islamic calendar started with *Hijra* (migration) of the Prophet SAW from Makkah to Madinah in the year 622 CE (Common Era). It is designated in English as AH (after *Hijra*), or just H, e.g., 80 AH meant 80 years after the Prophet's migration to Madinah, which was the year 702 CE. Of note, Prophet SAW passed away in the year 11AH, 11 years after migrating to Madinah.

- **Hanafi School of Thought**
  - By Imam Abu **Hanifa** al-Nauman bin Thabit bin Zuta bin Marzuban (RA)
  - 80 AH Kufa to 150 AH Baghdad

- **Ja'fari School of Thought**
  - By Imam **Ja'far** ibn Muhammad as-Sadiq (RA)
  - 83 AH to 148 AH Madinah

- **Maliki School of Thought**
  - By Imam **Malik** ibn Anas (RA)
  - 93 AH to 179 AH Madinah

- **Isma'ili School of Thought**
  - Imam Abu Muhammad **Isma'il** ibn Ja'far (RA)
  - 103 AH to 138 AH Madinah
- **Shafi School of Thought**
  - By Imam Abu Abdullah Muhammad ibn Idris al-**Shafi (RA)**
  - 150 AH Gaza to 204 AH Egypt

- **Hanbali School of Thought**
  - Imam Abu Abdillah Ahmad ibn Muhammad ibn **Hanbal** Ash-Shaybani (RA)
  - 164 AH to 241 AH Baghdad

- **Zahiri School of Thought**
  – Imam Dawud bin Ali bin Khalaf al-**Zahir (RA)**
  – 199 AH Isfahan to 270 AH Baghdad

The above list is compiled to make a point that even within the general principles of Islam described in previous pages, difference of opinion in religious interpretations and understanding was a part of Islam. Ignoring this fact promotes exclusiveness and has been counterintuitive to the larger concept of Islamic *Ummah*. This treatise does not address the reasons of why and how different Islamic schools of thought originated, or their differences. These topics are important and interesting and need a separate analysis. But for the benefit of a reader not versed with this subject, in the following paragraphs, I have provided an overview.

In general, the way I noted, all the above schools accepted the Quran in its original form and rightful position. They also accepted Prophet Muhammad SAW as the last prophet of Allah SWT, and his final authority in religious matters. The difference of opinion was mostly about issues and situations without any clear reference or guidance in the Quran or the *Hadith*, in which case opinion(s) of someone other than the Prophet SAW was considered. This principle was also based upon the Quran:

The Quran, Al-Nisa, *ayah* 115 (Al-Quran 4:115):

> "If anyone contends with the Messenger even after guidance has been plainly conveyed to him, and follows a path other than that becoming to **men of Faith**, We shall leave him in the path he has chosen, and land him in the Hell – what an evil refuge!" Ali.

> "And whoever contradicts and opposes the Messenger (Muhammad SAW) after the right path has been shown clearly to him, and follows other than **the believers'** way. We shall keep him in the path he has chosen, and burn him in Hell – what an evil destination." Al-Hilali & Khan.

Though agreeing with the principle, people differ about who the "believers" or the "men of Faith" could be? Who may be included in this group, and consulted for any question or clarification not directly or unequivocally addressed in the Quran and the *Hadith*? This disagreement started early on resulting in diverging points of view. The most conservative position is to avoid any opinion other than what is in the Quran, and the *Hadith* (of note, anyone only accepting the Quran, and not the *Hadith*, is in contradiction, and not following either of them). Some people respect and follow the first generation, though there are differences within that group too. Another group accepts opinion(s) of later early generation(s), and yet many others, while formulating or obtaining an opinion, do not restrict themselves to any generation or the time.

When trying to explain an issue, like *Riba*, scholars of different schools try to achieve the same goal; they try to follow the principles of the Quran, and the words and actions of the Prophet SAW. Also, in general, there is almost no difference of opinion in matters clearly mentioned in the Quran. For example, based upon its injunction in the Quran, all the above schools agree that meat of swine is *haram* or generally not allowed for eating. I am not aware of any specific *hadith* about this matter. So, for this matter, the words of the Quran are deemed satisfactorily clear and sufficient.

Each School of Thought listed above accept the validity of the words of the Quran as we may see today. But the issue of translation and interpretation of the Quran is a different matter. The subject of differences in the interpretation of the Quran between different schools is also quite large and not addressed in this writing. In brief, I compiled the following list (probably partial) of factors resulting in variations in the translation or interpretation, (and *Tafsir* or *Tawil*) of the Quran:

1: Variation of meaning of a word

2: Variation of meaning of an *ayah*, sometimes based upon its delivery (recitation)

3: Time and occasion of revelation

4: Ancient historical context

5: The relevant *hadith* of Prophet SAW, if available and/or agreed upon

6: Analysis without context, e.g., ancient history, time-period, occasion of revelation, etc.

7: Allegorical analysis

8: Opinion of the first generation of Muslims

9 Opinion of scholars or the Imams

10: Locational (the location of an ayah or a *surah* in the Quran) analysis

11: Mathematical analysis

In one way or the other, and in general, every above listed school tried to use the same principles to reach an opinion on any religious matter. The difference amounted to the weightage given to different aspects of this decision-making process. Following is a brief overview of the approach taken by each school:

***Hanafi* School of Thought:** This school is influenced by Imam Abu **Hanifa** al-Nauman bin Thabit bin Zuta bin Marzuban (80 AH Kufa to 150 AH Baghdad), may Allah SWT be pleased with him. Imam Abu Hanifa gained respect and repute due to his deep knowledge and understanding of the fundamentals of religion (the Quran and the *Hadith*), and its application to provide answers for peoples' problems. As per history available to us, at one point in his life, he was asked by the ruler of that time to lead the justice department (the *Qadi* system), which he declined. It was impossible and not important for us to figure out the ruler's intention to hire him, and the Imam's reasons for refusal. Despite lack of any official position, he was deeply respected by his peers and the masses, and his interpretations and juristic principles flourished exponentially after his death. The system, or the *fiqh*, he influenced was ultimately adopted by the state and later became known as the *Hanafi* way, or the *Hanafi fiqh* or School of thought. It was also the oldest of these schools and accepted by more Muslims in the world than any other. Through the Ottoman's rule in "the West" and the Mughals in "the East", and their adoption of this system, its influence extended to the largest areas of Muslim rule.

For a *Hanafi* scholar or a jurist, the foremost source for any opinion is the Quran, followed by the *Hadith*, if there are specific and pertinent instructions in it. If these two sources do not provide a clear answer, the scholar is allowed a juristic analysis or *ijtihad*. There are multiple levels of analysis, some stricter than others, depending upon the question in hand. After exhausting any previous opinions (like the opinion of the first generation of Muslims), the cornerstone of juristic analysis is *Qias*, reasoning by analogy. Precedents are generally followed but, in some situations, depending upon the nature and significance of the matter, a jurist is allowed to ignore a precedent and reach a different conclusion by using an alternate analogy, i.e., the concept of *istihsan* or approbation. Compared to many others, the *Hanafi* School is a relatively "liberal and progressive" system.

***Ja'fari* School of Thought:** This is influenced by Imam **Ja'far** ibn Muhammad as-Sadiq (83 AH to 148 AH Madinah), may Allah SWT be pleased with him. Despite lack of writings, which can be reliably attributed to him, it is generally understood that Imam Ja'far was responsible to develop a religious doctrine, somewhat different from the ones of his time (the *Hanafi* and the *Maliki*), which ultimately became the source of the Shia doctrines or Shia *fiqhs*. It is the official *fiqh* of present-day Iran. In Ja'fari *fiqh*, comparatively speaking, there is larger emphasis on *ijtihad* or juristic analysis. The scholar or the *mujtahid*, who is considered a representative of the Imam, who himself is considered a representative of the Prophet SAW, has larger flexibility to make decisions. While the general principles of the Quran and the *Hadith* are followed, there is larger flexibility to consider variables such as the specific time period, location or the venue, and the situation. In many ways, it is even more liberal than the *Hanafi* School. Also, there are many distinct theological and practical differences between the *Ja'fari* School, as understood by the contemporary Shia scholars, and the "Sunni" *fiqhs*, e.g., the concept of the highest juristic or interpretive authority residing with the Imam in the *Ja'fari* system.

Maliki **School of Thought**: This school is influenced by Imam **Malik** ibn Anas (93 AH to 179 AH Madinah), may Allah SWT be pleased with him. This is like the *Hanafi* School, relying on the Quran and the Hadith as the basic source of the Law. If required, varying degrees of juristic analysis is allowed. The difference is the higher relative value given to the consensus of the early residents or scholars of Madinah.

Isma'ili **School of Thought:** This school is influenced by Imam Abu Muhammad **Isma'il** ibn Ja'far (103 AH to 138 AH Madinah), may Allah SWT be please with him. This is one of the many Shia Schools, accepting Imam Isma'il ibn Ja'far as the spiritual figurehead. Like any other Shia *fiqh*, the present Imam retains religious authority over any other contemporary scholar.

Shafi **School of Thought**: This school is influenced by Imam Abu Abdullah Muhammad ibn Idris al-**Shafi** (150 AH Gaza to 204 AH Egypt), may Allah SWT be pleased with him, who was a student of Imam Malik ibn Anas RA. His teachings, and writings helped influence the development of this school. Probably the main difference between this and the other schools is the particular emphasis on the authenticated a*hadith* and *Sunnah* of the Prophet Muhammad SAW, and avoidance of the opinions of the narrators or the scholars. Subsequently, at times, an opinion by a Shafi scholar may be more 'conservative' than the *Hanafi* or the *Maliki fiqh*.

Hanbali School of Thought: This school is influenced by Imam Abu Abdillah Ahmad ibn Muhammad ibn **Hannibal** AshShaybani (164 AH to 241 AH Baghdad), may Allah SWT be pleased with him. This is considered the most conservative of the conventionally known "Sunni" schools of thought. It is debatable though, if Imam ibn Hanbal himself provided the framework presently attributed to this school. In general, opinions in this *fiqh* are obtained from the principles outlined in the Quran and the *Hadith*. If needed, opinions of the first generation of Muslims are respected and accepted, but there is less room for further juristic analysis. Variations of this *fiqh* are practiced in present-day Saudi Arabia, Qatar, and a few other countries in that area.

Zahiri School of Thought: This school was influenced by Imam Dawud bin Ali bin Khalaf al-**Zahir (**199 AH Isfahan to 270 AH Baghdad), may Allah SWT be pleased with him. The distinctive feature of this school was emphasis on the literal meaning of the Quran and the *Hadith*, and rejection of *qias* or analogical reasoning. In this manner, it was somewhat closer to the *Hanbali* School. In places influenced by this school, such as Andalusia, some other schools, such as *Maliki*, were outlawed and rejected. After the demise of Muslim rule in Andalusia, this school mostly lost its significance. Did this school contribute to the demise of Muslim rule in Spain? This is an interesting topic but not related to the subject matter of this book.

What shall one do then – especially the one new to Islam or learning it afresh – with all these different schools of thought?
The usually given answer to this question, in some accommodating circles, is that one may follow any of these

schools, or even, to a certain extent, pick and choose when looking for an opinion on a particular matter. Unfortunately, this suggestion is, a. Somewhat impractical, as most people lack the resources or the ability to review different opinions, and b. In practice, it is discouraged by the religious leaders who seldom agree to or provide an alternate of the viewpoint of their choice. This issue is the major factor contributing to the divisions and conflicts within Muslim society. The divisions did not just stop with the above-described schools of thought, there are further sub-divisions within the followers of these schools.

Humans are a tribal animal, and it is very difficult for any human being to deviate from their ancestor's beliefs and traditions, whatever they might be. Islamic perspective on this is explained by these two *ayat* of the Quran, about the problem of following wrong traditions of ancestors, and the fundamental Islamic principle that all of us are responsible and accountable for our own self.

The Quran, Al-Maidah, *ayah* 104-105 (Al-Quran 5:104-105)

> "When it is said to them: "Come to what Allah hath revealed; come to the messenger"; they say: "Enough for us are the ways we found our fathers following." What! Even though their fathers were void of knowledge and guidance? O ye who believe! Guard your own souls: if ye follow (right) guidance, no hurt can come to you from those who stray. The goal of you all is to Allah: it is He that will show you the truth of all that ye do." Ali.

> "And when it is said to them: "Come to what Allah has revealed and unto the Messenger

(Muhammad SAW for the verdict of that which you have made unlawful)." They say: "Enough for us is that which we found our fathers following," even though their fathers had no knowledge whatsoever and no guidance. O you who believe! Take care of your ownselves, [do righteous deeds, fear Allah much (abstain from all kinds of sins and evil deeds which He has forbidden) and love Allah much (perform all kinds of good deeds which He has ordained)]. If you follow the right guidance and enjoin what is right (Islamic Monotheism and all that Islam orders one to do) and forbid what is wrong (polytheism, disbelief and all that Islam has forbidden) no hurt can come to you from those who are in error. The return of you all is to Allah, then He will inform you about (all) that which you used to do." Al-Hilali & Khan.

These *ayat* are typically read as they are addressing the issues of non-Muslims, but their application is universal, including to the ones deviated within the "Muslim" community.

What may be helpful is to understand the basics of Islam as described earlier, especially its intellectual basis, and avoid exclusively gravitating towards, or adopting a particular school of thought, or identifying with one. Islamic history is full of discords and fights, both intellectual and physical, triggered by zealous preference of one of the above schools of thought, or their derivation, over other(s). Mosques and Islamic institutions are better off not identifying themselves, explicitly or implicitly, with any such school or their derivations, while studying and reflecting on all of them. Logically speaking, any mosque or an Islamic institution identifying itself in that manner is promoting an exclusionary concept, which is inherently counterintuitive to the basic principles of Islam.

CHAPTER 9

THE CONCEPT OF JURISTIC ANALYSIS

The cornerstone of juristic analysis or *Ijtihad* is the concept of **reasoning by analogy, *qias*.** After reviewing the Quran and the *Hadith*, and after exhausting the opinions of the companions of the Prophet SAW, the Al-Shafi school allows relying upon reasoning by analogy. The *Hanafi* School, on the other hand also allows **approbation (*istihsan*)**, when a jurist may ignore an established law or a precedent and approve an alternate argument for a good or merciful reason, but still using the principles outlined in the Quran and the *Hadith*. The *Maliki* School allows **benefit-analysis (*istislah*)**, and sometimes accommodation due to **local customs ('*urf*)**. For a Shafi scholar any opinion other than *qias*, reasoning by analogy, may be invalid. The *Hanbali* School, like the *Zahiri* school, is stricter, relying on the Quran, *Hadith* and *Sunnah* of the Prophet SAW, and opinion of the *Sahabah* or companions of the Prophet SAW, and may not accept any other juristic interpretation or clarification. The *Ja'fari* School seems most liberal of all, somewhat closer to the *Maliki* point of view, with larger significance given to the opinion of an Imam, but in a manner not very different from a *Mujtahid* in Sunni Islam with broader freedom for a jurist to consider multiple factors before reaching a decision, such as time, place, and circumstances. It is important to mention that the modern day Islamic financial instruments, documentation and practices are mainly designed using the concept of *istislah*, the benefit-analysis.

Legal contents of the Quran such as the subject of *Riba*, because of its significance and complex nature, or because of the way it is generally understood, requires further explanation and clarifications. The Quran clearly mentions that *Riba* is not allowed but aside from some clear-cut cases, very little is mentioned about what exactly *Riba* is. This may have been the reason that even within early Muslims, understanding of *Riba* in some situations required corrections or clarifications from the Prophet SAW. After the Prophet SAW passed away and without his correcting or clarifying authority the situation became more difficult. During the first four caliphates, each of the four caliphs, may Allah SWT be pleased with them, was taken as religious authority. There was ample evidence though to suggest that they made decisions or proclamations after consultation or *shura* with many important and/or relevant people, both men and women. Following narration in the Musnad of Imam Hanbal RA was such an example:

Musnad Imam Ahmad bin Hanbal, Musnad Umar bin Al-Khattab, 82: It was narrated that Haritha said: Some people from Syria came to 'Umar and said: we have acquired wealth and horses and slaves, and we want to pay *zakat* on them as a purification. He said: I shall do what my two predecessors did. He consulted the Companions of Muhammad SAW, among whom was Ali, and Ali said: It is good, provided it does not become a regular tax that is taken from them after you are gone.

The issue of lack of full clarity about *Riba,* at least in some situations, which was noted even when Prophet SAW was alive, continued during the 3rd phase, an important period in Muslim intellectual history when almost all major religious schools of thought came about. This issue continues to this day, getting more complicated with time, as some newer or more complex financial tools and means are developed. Religious injunctions or rules for a concept like *Riba* are deduced based upon what is understood from the Quran, the *Hadith* and *Sunnah* of the Prophet SAW, opinion of the companions of the Prophet (or the scholars), or an Imam (for *Ja'afari* school), and finally, if the matter required any further clarification, the juristic analysis.

Islamic governance starting from the first caliph to the end of the Ottoman's rule did not have the concept of political opposition, as one might understand this term in a modern and/or democratic way of governance. After the 2nd Phase or after the caliphate of the first four caliphs, in practical terms, the election of a ruler and the rule of governance were autocratic. Difference of opinion within the Muslim communities prevailed and was relatively tolerated, but only relatively, and more so in the religious sphere than the political. This was rooted in the differentiations of religious understandings or interpretations of the sacred text. People followed an Imam or a scholar of their choice, usually promoted by the contemporary ruler, e.g., implementation of

Imam Abu Hanifa's jurisprudence in certain parts of the Muslim rule, and of Imam Malik in others, both ordained through injunctions by the respective rulers of their times. One might find similar patterns and practices in other Muslim communities. The concept of *Riba* was a key component of Islamic jurisprudence and its rulings were intertwined with business contracts and practices.

Before going into the specifics of juristic analysis about *Riba* and Islamic finance, the following three chapters provide details of what is mentioned about *Riba* in previous scriptures, the Quran, and the *Hadith*.

CHAPTER 10

RIBA IN ANCIENT CIVILIZATIONS AND PREVIOUS SCRIPTURES

Charging a borrower an amount, which frequently was abusive, in addition to the principal amount lent has been a centuries old practice. One may find many terms or names for this practice, such as "usury" and "interest" in English language. In Hinduism, a civilization not based upon Abrahamic faith, its practice was mostly allowed and any of its restrictions were either limited or applied only to certain castes. Anyone interested in more detail may refer to this article: https://www.islam-hinduism.com/usury-in-hinduism-and-islam-1-2/.

Aristotle argued against usury, comparing money with food material (which was not rented), and the fact that, unlike assets like real estate or animals (maybe an automobile for present day comparison), the money did not produce anything. Like food, it was a fungible (mutually interchangeable) item, and once used, it needed replacement. On the other hand, the real estate or animals were

The Islamic Finance and the Riba

not fungible, could be used to make money, e.g., by renting. Their use did not make them disappear, and each one of them had a unique value. The food had to be eaten or the money had to be spent to gain any benefit from it. It was considered either unethical or illogical to charge an additional amount while lending food or money, the fungible items.

Following was a reference from a Buddhism text:
> "One discerns wrong livelihood as wrong livelihood, and right livelihood as right livelihood. And what is wrong livelihood? Scheming, persuading, hinting, belittling, and charging interest. This is wrong livelihood." Siddharta Gautama Buddha in his sermon on the Eightfold Path (Majjhima Nikaya Suttra 117).

Ancient China was influenced by multiple philosophies, including Confucianism and Buddhism, beside some others. It seemed that in ancient Chinese societies there was no law forbidding usury but there was some evidence that the governments or authorities tried to minimize its impact to the poor or the farmers, by providing loans with minimum or zero interest.

Romans allowed usury but with some controls. They tried to set a limit to the highest amount of interest one could charge. They also legislated a different set of rates for different uses, e.g., lower rates for farmers and highest for someone financing foreign voyages.

Under Abrahamic faith, it was prohibited for Jews, but with a caveat of allowance while dealing with non-Jews, or that was the way many understood it. Jews were severely discriminated in pre-modern Europe, and at times they relied more on professions, which Christians around them did not adopt such as moneylending. Old Christian societies made usury illegal. At times, people charging usury were either severely punished or even killed. The practice of lending money with interest was not without controversy within Jewish circles either. Some Jewish religious voices considered Christians and Muslims following the same Abrahamic principles and did not agree on charging them interest. One may find similar stories of Sikhs and Hindus of Afghanistan, or northwestern Pakistan, living in conservative Muslim societies. In historical terms, allowing or charging interest on a loan within Christian societies is a relatively recent concept.

Another aspect of this historic subject is that, until recently, moneylending was mostly between individuals, with little legislative control and without direct involvement of an institution like a bank. From the Islamic perspective, there was no historical evidence of a societal control over its conduct in the pre-Islamic Arabia or the early Islamic society (before the *ayat* for its prohibitions were revealed). Individuals were free to charge whatever suited them. There have been some relatively recent examples of similar individual-based lending systems, in Afghanistan, Pakistan, and India. The practice of individual-control or without-control lending system was particularly unfair and abusive to the borrower. Regulatory development of the modern banking system in Christian Europe where it was previously curtailed was, in a way, an effort towards providing an alternate or a 'fair' system of money-borrowing and lending.

Riba, understood as usury, was a well-known concept and practice within ancient Jewish societies, as it was during most of the life of the Prophet Muhammad SAW, until the *ayah* about its prohibition was revealed. Following were some of the references about usury in the Jewish scripture:

> Psalm 15:5. Those who lend money without charging interest, and who cannot be bribed to lie about the innocent. Such people will stand firm forever.
>
> Exodus 22:25. If you loan money to my people, to the poor among you, don't be like a creditor to them and don't impose interest on them.
>
> Deuteronomy 23:19. Do not charge a fellow Israelite interest, whether on money or food or anything else that may earn interest. You may charge a foreigner interest, but not a fellow Israelite, so that the Lord your God may bless you in everything you put your hand to in the land you are entering to possess.
>
> Leviticus 25: 36-37. Do not take interest or any profit from them, but fear your God, so that they may continue to live among you. You must not lend them money at interest or sell them food at a profit.
>
> Ezekiel 18:13. he lends *money* on interest and takes increase; will he live? He will not live! He has committed all these abominations; he will surely be put to death; his blood will be on his own head.

The first two references in the Psalm and the Exodus affirmed piety of lending money without interest, while discouraging charging interest to poor. The next two references in Deuteronomy and Leviticus again discouraged this practice but allowed it while dealing with non-Jews. The strongest statement against usury was from the book of Ezekiel but for many Jews it was a controversial book, and generally not included in the basic set of five books of Torah. Based upon the reference in Deuteronomy 23:19, Jewish practice of lending money with interest while dealing with non-Jews might be a valid excuse for them, if they were not charging it to their own faith members. Another point to ponder was about the latter part of the statement in Leviticus, "You must not lend them money at interest or sell them food at a profit." In today's rapidly urbanizing world, it was impractical to expect that every consumer could grow his own food or could have access to a producer of food. Complex food supply chains existed in every society without which reliable supply of food was impractical, and which could not function without expectation of profit taking at every transaction.

For Christians, the above statements of the Old Testament are still valid. There was apparently no specific restriction on usury mentioned in the New Testament. Within Christian religious scholars there is difference of opinion about usury, especially about its definition, i.e., whether it implied a "fair charge" for the lent money or the excessive or abusive charge. This is reflected in the variety of translations, and following is such an example:

Ezekiel 18:13

1. And charges interest and takes [a percentage of] increase on what he has loaned; will he then live? He will not live! He has done all these disgusting things, he shall surely be put to death; his blood will be on his own head. Amplified Bible.

2. He lends money for interest and makes excessive profits. Will this person live? He will not live. He has done all these disgusting things. So he must die, and he will be responsible for his own death. God's WORD translation.

3. He lends *money* on interest and takes increase; will he live? He will not live! He has committed all these abominations; he will surely be put to death; his blood will be on his own head. New American Standard Bible 1995.

In recent times, most Christian religious authorities, including Catholics, have sanctified at least some or "fair" charge or interest on lending money.

CHAPTER 11

WHAT IS IN THE QURAN ABOUT RIBA?

A*yat* of the Quran related to the subject of *Riba* were revealed during the last part of the Quranic revelation. As one may notice, these *ayat* do not provide details of *Riba*, their emphasis is mostly on its prohibition. For this chapter where the primary subject is the *ayat* of the Quran, instead of two, five different versions of its translation are provided. These translations are picked partly because they were originally written in English. They represent multiple historical time frames, and a variety of the English language, including its old, contemporary, and American versions. English re-translation of the translation of the Quran from other languages is avoided to minimize error and confusion, but a number of those translations are otherwise reviewed, including many written in Urdu language.

Following five translations are included in this chapter:

1. **The Meaning of the Glorious Koran** by Muhammad Marmaduke **Pickthall** (1875-1936)

2. **The Meaning of the Holy Quran** by Abudullah Yusuf **Ali** (1872-1953).

3. **The Noble Qur'an by** Dr. Muhammad Taqi-ud-Din **Al-Hilali**, PH.D. (1893-1987) & Dr. Muhammad Muhsin **Khan** (1927-2021).

4. **The Meanings of The Noble Qur'an** by Mufti Muhammad Taqi **Usmani** (1943-).

5. **The Gracious Quran** by Ahmad Zaki **Hammad** (published in 2007).

There are multiple *ayat* of the Quran with reference to the concept of *Riba*. They are as follows, not in any particular order:

1. The Quran, Al-Nisa, *ayah* 161 (Al-Quran 4:161).

This reference of *Riba* is about its practice by some Jews, while reminding them that their scripture did not approve it (see Exodus 22: 25, and Leviticus 25: 36-37).

The translation of this and the preceding *ayah* is as follows:

> a. "Because of the wrongdoing of the Jews We forbade them good things which were (before) made lawful unto them, and because of their much hindering from Allah's way, And of their taking usury when they were forbidden it, and of their devouring people's wealth by false pretenses, We

have prepared for those of them who disbelieve a painful doom." Pickthall.

b. "For the iniquity of the Jews We made unlawful for them certain (foods) good and wholesome which had been lawful for them; in that they hindered many from Allah's way. That they took usury, though they were forbidden; and that they devoured men's substance wrongfully; We have prepared for those among them who reject Faith a grievous punishment." Ali.

c. "For the wrong-doing of the Jews, We made unlawful for them certain good foods which has been lawful for them, and for their hindering many from Allah's Way; And their taking of *Riba* (usury) though they were forbidden from taking it and their devouring of men's substance wrongfully (bribery). And We have prepared for the disbelievers among them a painful torment." Al-Hilali & Khan.

d. "And for their charging Riba (usury or interest) while they were forbidden from it, and for their devouring of the properties of the people by false means. We have prepared, for the disbelievers among them, a painful punishment." Usmani.

e. "And for their taking 'of' usury, though they were forbidden to do it; and for their consuming the wealth of the people by false means. Moreover, We have prepared for the disbelievers among them a most painful torment 'in the Hereafter'." Hammad.

This *ayah* is referencing *Riba* as practiced by some Jews, which conflicted with what was mentioned in the scripture (see the references in the previous chapter). For the believers, it is providing a historical correction. It is not specifically describing an injunction of *Riba* for Muslims but rather the history of its practice within the Jewish community. Other than that, it is important to make a note that unlike all other translations, Usmani has added the word "interest" with usury, a significant addition, and a subject I discuss later.

2. The Quran, Al-Rum, *ayah* 39 (Al-Quran 30:39).

   a. "That which ye give in usury in order that it may increase on (other) people's property hath no increase with Allah; but that which ye give in charity, seeking Allah's Countenance, hath increase manifold." Pickthall.

   b. "That which ye lay out for increase through the property of (other) people, will have no increase with Allah; but that which ye give for charity, seeking the Countenance of Allah (will increase): it is these who will get a recompense multiplied." Ali.

   c. "And that which you give in gift (to others), in order that it may increase (your wealth by expecting to get a better one in return) from other people's property, has no increase with Allah; but that which you give in Zakat (sadaqa – charity etc.) seeking Allah's countenance then those, they shall have manifold increase." Al-Hilali & Khan.

d. "Whatever Riba (increased amount) you give, so that it may increase it in the wealth of the people, it does not increase with Allah: and whatever Zakah you give, seeking Allah's pleasure with it, (it is multiplied by Allah, and) it is such people who multiply (their wealth in real terms.)" Usmani.

e. "Yet 'beware, for' whatever you give 'others' in usury – to 'gain' increase from the wealth of people – shall never increase with God! But 'blessed is' whatever you give of the Zakat – Charity – desiring 'only' the Face of God. For it is such as these who shall have a 'much' multiplied reward." Hammad.

As noted, aside from the linguistic differences, there is variance of opinion about this *ayah's* translation and interpretation. The difference of opinion is mainly about the meaning of the word *'riba'* in the first part of the *ayah*. The literal meaning of this word is 'increase', or 'gain'. Many translated it as a gift one may give to someone with expectation of a reward or increase in their own wealth, while some translated it as 'usury' or the forbidden *Riba*. The scholars who preferred the second viewpoint, translating it as usury, seem to be relying either on the historical understanding of this concept, or its literal meaning, while ignoring the context.

If one takes the word *riba* in this ayah as usury, as Pickthall or Hammad did, it seems not to make overall sense. Usury was an ancient well-understood financial concept. For its giver, it was neither an investment nor a gift, and was generally given under duress. It is illogical for the giver of usury to expect a reward or increase in his/her wealth, which this *ayah* is referencing. Some scholars, instead of translating or using an explanatory term, just repeated the word *Riba*. For example, Usmani avoided translating it, and mentioned the word *Riba* as it was, with its literal understanding in brackets (increased amount). The reader is left without clarity of what the translator or the *ayah* meant.

This *ayah* is referencing something that is willingly given with expectation of a reward and is called *Riba*. It only made sense if one understands the full or expanded meaning of the concept of *Riba*, instead of merely calling it usury or illegal increase. So was the case, likely, that Ali and Al-Hilali & Khan avoided translating it as usury or repeating the word *Riba*, instead they tried to provide translation or an explanatory term that made overall sense of what is stated in the *ayah*. Their approach seems to make better sense. To understand the subject matter of this *ayah*, especially its context, I find it helpful to first read the previous two *ayat*. Following is the translation of these three *ayat* together (two versions are provided):

> "See they not that Allah enlarges the provision and restricts it, to whomsoever He pleases? Verily in that are Signs for those who believe. So give what is due to kindred, the needy, and the wayfarer. That is best for those who seek the Countenance of Allah and it is they who will prosper. That which ye lay out for increase through the property of (other) people, will have no increase with Allah; but that which ye give for charity, seeking the Countenance of Allah (will increase): it is these who will get a recompense multiplied." Ali.

> "Do they not see that Allah enlarges the provision for whom He wills and straitens (it for whom He wills). Verily, in that are indeed signs for a people who believe. So give to the kindred his due, and to the poor, and to the wayfarer; that is best for those who seek Allah's Countenance, and it is they who will be successful. And that which you give in gift (to others), in order that it may increase (your wealth by expecting to get a better one in return) from other people's property, has no increase with Allah; but that which you give in Zakat (*sadaqa* – charity etc.) seeking Allah's countenance, then those, they shall have manifold increase." Al-Hilali & Khan.

In this ayah, Allah SWT is comparing two types of giving, one given as charity to poor, needy, travelers, etc., and the other as a gift to a rich person, a government official, a successful businessman, etc.

In the first case, nothing in return is expected from the one receiving it, and any reward is expected from Allah SWT.

In the second type, a reward or benefit is expected from a human being or an entity other than Allah SWT. So, based upon these *ayat*, giving or gifting someone with the intention, expectation or hope of a reward or increase in one's own wealth (e.g., by getting favors from the other party) does not have Allah SWT's blessing. Increase and reward from Allah SWT is for the one giving charity and the *Zakat*.

A simple example to explain this type of giving is what we call commercial bribery, or a gift given to an official, a rich, or an influential person with hope of a contract, a business opportunity, or any such (illegal or unethical) reward. And this type of giving is classified as the *Riba*. This ayah throws light on the expansive concept of *Riba* in Islam, more than interest or usury. Concepts of interest or usury are applicable to a loan, which is not the subject matter of this *ayah*. Only Allah SWT knows best.

3. The Quran, Al-Imran, *ayah* 130 (Al-Quran 3:130).

   a. "O ye who believe! Devour not usury, doubling and quadrupling (the sum lent). Observe your duty to Allah, that ye may be successful." Pickthall.

   b. "O ye who believe! Devour not usury, doubled and multiplied; but fear Allah; that ye may (really) prosper." Ali.

   c. "O you who believe! Eat not *Riba* (usury) doubled and multiplied, but fear Allah that you may be successful." Al-Hilali & Khan.

   d. "O you who believe, do not eat up the amounts acquired through *Riba* (interest), doubled and multiplied. Fear Allah, so that you may be successful." Usmani.

   e. "O you who believe! You shall not consume usury 'on anything lent', multiplying and compounding 'the return', rather, be ever God-fearing, so that you may be successful." Hammad.

Again, noted in the above translation is repetition of the word *Riba* (with intended meaning in brackets) instead

Chapter 11 – What Is in The Quran About Riba?

of providing a translation pertinent to the *ayah*. The *Riba* in this ayah is generally understood as the usury, with its historical abusive connotation. Translating it as 'interest', as by Usmani, is problematic. Interest, as understood in financial terms and in comparison, to usury, is a relatively modern concept. Depending upon its terms, it may or may not reach a level of what we call usury. It is important to be clear and precise about the concepts of usury and interest, and especially to know if they are the same or two different concepts. Is it correct to interchange the word usury for *Riba*? Before addressing this subject, it is important to mention that the purpose of the following analysis is not to prove that interest cannot be *Riba*, or not *haram*; the purpose is exactitude, as much as possible.

In literature, usury is defined as follows:

Oxford Dictionary: The practice of lending money to people at unfairly high rates of interest.

Merriam-Webster Dictionary: 1. The lending of money with an interest charge for its use. 2. An unconscionable or exorbitant rate or amount of interest. 3. Interest.

Wikipedia: The practice of making unethical or immoral monetary loans that unfairly enriches the lender.

Overall, the commonly understood meaning of usury is closer to what is alluded to in the above *ayah*, an unreasonable charge on the amount lent.

As stated before, usury was an ancient practice that was rejected and prohibited in the Old Testament and the Quran. If the modern-day interest is the same thing, why do we not call it usury? Aside from the linguistic matter of their names or the terms used (interest or usury) we can try to find out their exact nature.

Concepts of interest and usury are alike in a way that they reflect a charge, an additional amount paid by the borrower to the lender. But, as understood, they are also different in the sense that modern day 'interest' is mostly (though not in all situations) regulated by governments through financial principles and instruments, based upon market conditions. Governments of financially stable and successful countries discourage and regulate charging more than what is fair and prohibit borrower abuse, while in some other relatively unregulated and less law-abiding societies, like Pakistan, interest rates are as abusive as any usury might be. This type of government operation is never perfect and requires constant vigilance to avoid exploitation and fraud. In addition, in societies not dictated by religious dictum, there is a struggle to balance the concept of free-market economy vs any control on the economy. The historical practice of usury, in comparison, was generally an unregulated, frequently abusive, mostly an individual- driven & controlled practice. The lender was able to charge any amount and could double or multiply it without any regulatory or legal repercussions.

Determination of interest rates in the modern banking system, or the banking system in the USA, is a complicated process. In general, bank rates are indirectly controlled by the government, through multiple types of tools and measures by the "central" bank and reflect the perceived or calculated market conditions. The central bank uses tools at its disposal to maximize monetary reward for the whole society and maintain a healthy and progressive economic environment. Fact that the

Chapter 11 – What Is in The Quran About Riba?

bank's interest rates are not arbitrary, and are based upon real-life market conditions, is also appreciated, and considered a valid benchmark by even the so-called Islamic banks. They use the same numbers to figure out "rate of profit" in the so-called *sharia*-compliant loan contracts, an interesting example of application of cost-benefit analysis, a *fiqh* concept.

In a system based upon usury, abuse was rampant and the borrower frequently lost big. On the other hand, in a system based upon a 'fair' interest, most borrowers benefit. There are multiple safeguards against borrower abuse. For example, in case of a default for a business or a project loan, personal life's essentials, such as the primary home or the car, are out of bounds. Liabilities are limited to the concerned business venture and/or the agreed upon collaterals, e.g., not more than the home in home financing or the car in auto financing. In such a system based upon controlled interest, if borrowers suffer, they suffer due to an act of nature or their own mistakes or greed, while in a system of usury, the lender inflicted most damage by taking undue advantage of the borrower's situation.

This *ayah* discourages excessive (double or multiplied) amount of usury. This is like a modern-day drive against abusive lending practice when a lender exploits a borrower by charging an exorbitant amount of interest and/or a shorter term to pay it off and/or excessive penalties and/or further increase in interest amount in case of a default.

4. The Quran, Al-Baqarah, *ayat* 275-276 (Al-Quran 2:275-276).

>   a. "Those who swallow usury cannot rise up save as he ariseth whom the devil hath prostrated

by (his) touch. That is because they say: Trade is just like usury; whereas Allah permitteth trading and forbiddeth usury. He unto whom an admonition from his Lord cometh, and (he) refraineth (in obedience thereto), he shall keep (the profits of) that which is past, and his affair (henceforth) is with Allah. As for him who returneth (to usury) – Such are rightful owners of the Fire. They will abide therein. Allah hath blighted usury and made almsgiving fruitful. Allah loveth not the impious and guilty." Pickthall.

b. "Those who devour usury will not stand except as stands one whom the Evil One by his touch hath driven to madness. That is because they say: "Trade is like usury," but Allah hath permitted trade and forbidden usury. Those who after receiving direction from their Lord, desist, shall be pardoned for the past; their case is for Allah (to judge); but those who repeat (the offence) are companions of the Fire: they will abide therin (for ever). Allah will deprive usury of all blessing, but will give increase for deeds of charity: for He loveth no creatures ungrateful and wicked." Ali.

c. "Those who eat *Riba* (usury) will not stand (on the Day of Resurrection) except like the standing of a person beaten by *Shaitan* (Satan) leading him to insanity. That is because they say: "Trading is only like *Riba* (usury)", whereas Allah has permitted trading and forbidden *Riba* (usury). So whosoever receives an admonition from his Lord and stops eating *Riba* (usury) shall not be punished for the past; his case is for Allah (to judge); but whoever returns [to *Riba* (usury)], such are the dwellers of the Fire – they will abide therein. Allah will destroy Riba (usury) and will give increase for sadaqat (deeds of charity, alms, etc.) And Allah likes not the disbelievers, sinners." Al-Hilali & Khan.

d. "Those who take Riba (usury or interest) will not stand but as stands the one whom demon has driven crazy by his touch. That is because they have said: "Sale is but like riba.", while Allah has permitted sale, and prohibited riba. So whoever receives an advice from his Lord and desists (from indulging in riba), then what has passed is allowed for him, and his matter is up to Allah. As for the ones who revert, those are the people of Fire. There they will remain forever. Allah destroys riba and nourishes charities, and Allah does not like any sinful disbeliever." Usmani.

e. "Those who devour usury shall not rise 'on Judgment Day', except as one rises whom Satan has battered with the touch 'of madness'. That is because they say: Indeed, selling is just like usury – while God has made selling lawful and has prohibited usury. So when an admonition comes to one from his Lord, and he quits 'usury', then to him belongs what was formerly 'gained'. And his affair 'henceforth' rests with God. But whoever returns 'to usury'– then these are the Companions of the Fire 'of Hell'. They shall abide therein forever. God obliterates 'all blessings from' usury and increases 'generously the reward for' charity. For God loves no relentlessly unbelieving sinner." Hammad.

The imagery of the day of resurrection about the fate of someone consuming *Riba* is particularly vivid, leaving no doubt about the gravity of this sin. A clear distinction is made between trading or business and the practice of *Riba*, the former clearly allowed and the later clearly forbidden. In a way, it is like stating that, in an Islamic system, prostitution or smuggling are not valid businesses or a form of trading and should not be practiced as such. Whosoever stop indulging in the practice of *Riba*, may not be punished, but whosoever not, shall be doomed to the Fire, living there forever. At the end, Allah SWT declares removal of His blessing from any income from the practice of *Riba*, while affirming it for charitable practices.

5. The Quran, Al-Baqrah, *ayat* 278-281 (Al-Quran 2:278-281).

   a. "O ye who believe! Observe your duty to Allah, and give up what remaineth (due to you) from usury, if ye are (in truth) believers. And if ye do not, then be warned of war (against you) from Allah and His messenger. And if ye repent, then ye have your principal (without interest). Wrong not, and ye shall not be wronged. And if the debtor is in straitened circumstances, then (let there be) postponement to (the time of) ease; and that ye remit the debt as almsgiving would be better for you if ye did but know." Pickthall.

   b. "O ye who believe! Fear Allah and give up what

Chapter 11 – What Is in The Quran About Riba?

remains of your demand for usury, if ye are indeed believers. If ye do it not, take notice of war from Allah and His Messenger: but if ye repent ye shall have your capital sums; deal not unjustly and ye shall not be dealt with unjustly. If the debtor is in a difficulty grant him time till it is easy for him to repay. But if ye remit it by way of charity, that is best for you if ye only knew." Ali.

c. "O you who believe! Be afraid of Allah and give up what remains (due to you) from *Riba* (usury) (from now onward), if you are (really) believers. And if you do not do it, then take a notice of war from Allah and His messenger, but if you repent, you shall have your capital sums. Deal not unjustly (by asking more than your capital sums), and you shall not be dealt with unjustly (by receiving less than your capital sums). And if the debtor is in a hard time (has no money), then grant him time till it is easy for him to repay, but if you remit it by way of charity, that is better for you if you did but know."Al-Hilali & Khan.

d. "O you who believe, fear Allah and give up what still remains of *riba*, if you are believers. But if you do not (give it up), then listen to the declaration of war of Allah and His Messenger. However, if you repent, yours is your principal. Neither wrong, nor be wronged. If there is one in misery, then (the creditor should allow) deferment till (his) ease, and that you forgo it as alms is much better for you, if you really know." Usmani.

e. "O you who believe! Be ever God-fearing and forsake all that remains 'due to you' from usury, if, indeed, you are believers. Yet if you do not do so, then be forewarned of war from God and His Messenger. But if you repent, for you is the capital of your wealth. You shall neither do wrong nor be wronged. Now, if one 'in debt' has hardship, then let there be respite, until there is ease 'for him'. And should you give it 'up' as charity, it is best for you, if you were to know." Hammad.

It is generally understood that these *ayat* were part of the last revelations the Prophet SAW received from Allah SWT. In these *ayat*, the practice of *Riba* was and is completely forbidden. People were and are asked to forgo any residual amount of *Riba* left in existing contracts, while reminding them of the covenant they made when they accepted Islam or considered themselves or declared to be Muslims. If the previous *ayat* or instructions from the Prophet SAW carried any doubt about illegality of *Riba*, these *ayat* made it abundantly clear with Allah SWT announcing a war against people who would continue to consume *Riba*.

These *ayat* should be read with the previous *ayat* described above where Allah SWT provides an imagery of the Hereafter and the plight and misfortune of someone consuming *Riba*. Despite the clarity of the message, the matter or the concept of Hereafter, for most of us, is somewhat difficult to comprehend. This may be the reason that people do not often change their day-to-day destructive or forbidden behavior. In these latter *ayat*, Allah SWT provides the description or the repercussions of a forbidden behavior, the practice of *Riba*, in the present worldly life. While one may consider that any repercussions in the hereafter is a far-off possibility, Allah SWT declares a war in this life against anyone consuming *Riba*. The war is something that may have its impact right away. Even thinking or planning about a war may have implications, but as soon as the war starts its destructive consequences start materializing. The message is straight-forward that the impact of the consumption of *Riba* for an individual, a family, or a society shall be immediate and like any war shall be ongoing, if the war continues.

The next part of the message provides instructions to end *Riba*-laden contracts, in a way also providing guideline to formulate *Riba*-free ones. The basis of this arrangement is described in four words, *"la tazlimoona wa la toozlamoon"*, deal not unjustly and you shall not be dealt with unjustly. Some scholars elaborate the concept of justice in this *ayah* by stating that the lender may have the original amount lent, but this explanation is not explicitly stated in this *ayah* and is debatable. I discuss this matter later in this discussion when I discuss the basis of *Riba*.

One of the fundamental concepts of Islam is justice, which in Islam always is associated with the concept of mercy, or *Ihsaan,* both in the matters related to an individual and Allah SWT, but especially in the matters related to one person with another, the *haqooqul-ibaad*, the matters or rights of the people. The matter of *Riba* as described in this latter part of *surah al-Baqarah* provides a glaring example of this principle. Right after elaborating the concept of justice between the lender and the borrower, *ihasaan* or the mercy is recommended for the borrowers not able to pay in time or not able to pay at all. *Ihsaan* or mercy for the deserving is always a preferable course of action in Islam, with its reward only expected from Allah SWT in this world and the hereafter.

This ends the details available in the Quran about the *Riba*. Despite multiple instructions, there is no explicit definition of *Riba* in the Quran, especially not in the manner one may understand it with help of the *Hadith*. This is a common theme in Islam about different practical matters, like *salat, siam,* or the *Hajj*. Details about these matters, and the *Riba*, are derived from the *Hadith* of the Prophet SAW, which is the subject matter of the next chapter.

CHAPTER 12

THE RIBA AND FINANCE IN THE HADITH LITERATURE

Unlike the Quran, there are numerous books of the *Hadith*, each one with somewhat varying contents. There is overlap when same or similar *ahadith* are mentioned in different books, but there also are differences when some a*hadith a*re only found in some texts and not others. There also is the matter of difference between two versions of the same book, especially in translated form. For example, I reviewed two translations of Sahih Bukhari: a. by Hilal Yayinlari and, b. by Dr. Muhammad Muhsin Khan. These two versions or translations at times differed in their contents, not every *hadith* mentioned in one translation (by Yahinlari) is found in the other (by Khan), which is a matter of remarkable consequences.

The subject of how one may address this issue of variance in the *Hadith* literature requires another discussion and is briefly touched elsewhere. In this chapter, an outline of references about the *Riba* in the *Hadith* literature is provided. Not every *hadith* about this subject is mentioned here as there is significant overlap or repetition of subject matter. It is not uncommon to note multiple narrators reporting the same or similar *hadith*. To avoid redundancy, instead of every documented *hadith* with a reference to *Riba*, an effort is made to include all related subject matter. Avoiding repetition, *ahadith* are listed based upon their subject matter. This approach may also help to better understand the subject of Islamic finance in general, and the *Riba* in particular, as mentioned in the *Hadith*.

Following is the subject list and related information in the *Hadith* literature:

What exactly is the *Riba*?

As mentioned above, the Quran, while providing categorical instructions about its prohibition, does not provide a full definition of *Riba*. I am not aware of any account in the *Hadith* or *Seerah* where someone explicitly asked the Prophet SAW about the concept of *Riba*, or he himself provided its explicit definition. The earliest documented account about this subject I was able to find is in the book, Al-Muwatta.

Al-Muwatta of Imam Malik ibn Anas of Madinah, may Allah SWT be pleased with him, is considered the first formal compilation of the *Hadith* literature, which was accomplished more than 100 years after the Prophet SAW passed away. The book is not just about the *Hadith*; it also contains opinions, mainly of the Imam Malik himself. In any case, this is considered the first formal 'book' of its kind, with a*hadith* compiled and categorized based upon subject matter. Compared to most other books of the *Hadith* written later, Al-Muwatta is a relatively small book, describing only 1,270 *ahadith*.

> Al-Muwatta Chapter 31.39: 83: Malik related to me (Imam Malik ibn Anas) that Zayd ibn Aslam said, "Usury in the *jahiliyya* was that a man would give a loan to a man for a set term. When the term was due, he would say, 'Will you pay it off or increase me?' If the man paid, he took it. If not, he increased him in his debt and lengthened the term for him."

This is an opinion statement, and not a *hadith* of the Prophet SAW. Its presence in the book implies at least two facts: a. There was a need to define *Riba*, even at that time, and b. There was no known *hadith* of the Prophet SAW about this subject. Otherwise, there was no need for Imam Malik to document this opinion. We may find later in the discussion that this definition is not enough to understand different types and aspects of *Riba*.

Following *ahadith* provided significant insight into the concept of *Riba*, though not its explicit definition:

> Sahih Al-Bukhari[2], Vol 3, XXXVIII, Chapter 11, 506. Narrated Abu Said al-Khudri RA: Once Bilal RA brought Barni (ie, a kind of dates) to the Prophet SAW and the Prophet asked him, "From where have you brought these?" Bilal replied, "I had some inferior type of dates and exchanged two Sa's of it for one Sa of Barni dates in order to give to the Prophet to eat." Thereupon the Prophet said, "Beware! Beware! This is definitely *Riba* (usury)! This is definitely *Riba* (usury)!

> Don't do so, but if you want to buy (a superior kind of dates) sell the inferior dates for money and then buy the superior kind of dates with that money."

Despite lack of any further detail, this probably is one of the most important *ahadith* to understand the concept of *Riba*. I provide further detail in the chapter where I discuss the fundamental nature of *Riba*.

> Sahih Al-Bukhari[3], Vol. 3, 2080: Narrated Abu Said RA: We used to be given mixed dates (from the booty) and used to sell (barter) two Sa (of those dates) for one Sa (of good dates). The Prophet SAW said (to us), "No (bartering of) two Sa, for one Sa, nor two Dirhams for one Dirham is permissible", [as that is a kind of Riba (usury)].

> Sunan Abu Dawud, Vol. 4, 3348: It was narrated that 'Umar said: "The Messenger of Allah SAW said: 'Gold for silver is *Riba* unless exchanged on the spot; wheat for wheat is *Riba* unless exchanged on the spot; dates for dates is *Riba* unless exchanged on the spot; and barley for barley is *Riba*, unless exchanged on the spot." *(Sahih)*

> Sunan Abu Dawud, Vol. 4, 3349. It was narrated from 'Ubādah bin As-Samit that the Messenger of Allah SAW said: "Gold for gold, pure or minted; silver for silver, pure or minted; wheat for wheat with equal measure; barley for barley with equal measure; dates for dates with equal measure; salt for salt with equal measure. Whoever gives more or asks for more has engaged in *Riba*. There is nothing wrong with selling gold for silver hand to hand, if

silver is more, but if it is on credit, then no. And there is nothing wrong with selling wheat for barley hand to hand, if barley is more, but if it is on credit, then no." *(Sahih)*

Following few *ahadith* provide evidence for the struggle understanding the concept of *Riba*, even within early generations of Muslims:

Sahih Al-Bukhari[2], Vol. 7, 493: Narrated Ibn Umar, 'Umar delivered a sermon on the pulpit of the Allah's Apostle SAW saying, "Alcoholic drinks were prohibited by Divine Order, and these drinks used to be prepared from five things, i.e., grapes, dates, wheat, barley or honey. Alcoholic drink is that, that disturbs the mind." Umar added, "I wish Allah's Apostle SAW had not left us before he had given us definite verdicts concerning three matters, i.e., how much a grandfather may inherit (of his grandson), the inheritance of *Al-Kalala* (the deceased person among whose heirs there is no father or son), and some type of *Riba* (usury)."

Al-Muwatta, Chapter 31.16: 37: Yahya related to me from Malik that Abu az-Zinad heard Said ibn al-Musayyab say, "There is usury only in gold or silver or what is weighed or measured of what is eaten or drunk."

Sahih Muslim Vol 4, Chapter 18, [4089] 102 – (. . .): It was narrated from Ubaidullah bin Abi Yazid that he heard Ibn Abbas say: "Usama bin Zaid told me that the Prophet SAW said: '*Riba* is only in the case of delayed payment.'"

The Islamic Finance and the Riba

> Sahih Muslim Vol 4, Chapter 18, [4090] 103 – (. . .): It was narrated from Ibn Abbas, from Usamah bin Zaid, that the Messenger of Allah SAW said: "There is no *Riba* in that which is hand to hand."

> Sahih Bukhari2, Vol. 3, Chapter 110, 430, page 237: Rafi bin Khadij once bought a camel for two camels and he delivered one instantly and said, "Allah willing, I will bring you the other tomorrow without delay." And said Ibn Al-Musaiyab, "There is no *Riba* (in animals), i.e., in selling one camel for two, or one sheep for two sheep on credit."

> Sahih Bukhari2, Vol. 3, Chapter 61: Ibn Abi Aufa said, "One who practices *Najsh* is a *Riba*-eating, traitor. And such a practice is a false trick which is forbidden, and the Prophet SAW said, 'Deception would lead to the Hell (Fire) and whoever does a deed which is not in accord with our tradition, then that deed will not be accepted.'"

> Sahih Bukhari[2], Vol. 3, 352: Narrated Ibn Umar RA, Allah's Apostle SAW forbade *Najsh*.

Najsh was described as to offer a high price for something without having the intention of buying it, and rather just to cheat somebody else who really wanted to buy. Aside from understanding the illegality of *Najsh* from this narration, one may also notice that the concept of *Riba*, as understood by some, was more than just an additional amount on a loan.

There are some additional narrations and *ahadith*, which have been quoted to provide significance of the sin of *Riba*. For example:

> Sunan ibn Majah, Vol. 3, 2274: It was narrated from Abu Hurairah that the Messenger of Allah SAW said: "There are seventy degrees of usury, . . . "

Many researchers and scholars have used this *hadith* to make a point about the danger of dealing with *Riba*. I find two issues with this notion: First, the Quran has already made it abundantly clear, with explicit wording and vivid description. And second, as far as this narration is concerned, out of respect for the Prophet SAW, I avoid completing the statement as recorded in the book. To me, it is disrespectful. This narration raises additional issues: First, understanding the nature and the character of the Prophet SAW, clearly evidenced from his dealings and statements, and in addition, vouched by the Quran, to accept that he used the kind of language reported in this narration, seems odd, if not unlikely. Even if we accept that this was his statement, it further raises the issue that the exact nature of *Riba* is not easy to decipher. On the other hand, the narration by no means provides any explanation about the nature of *Riba*. I address this issue, the fundamental nature of *Riba*, in detail in a later section.

Can a borrower pay or return more than what is lent?

This is not a straightforward question, as it has more than one dimension. Following is a related *hadith*, and an opinion of Imam Malik in Al-Muwatta:

> Sahih Al-Bukhari[2], Vol 3, 579: Narrated Jabir bin Abdullah RA: I went to the Prophet SAW while he was in the Mosque. After the Prophet told me to pray two *Rakat*, he paid me the debt he owed me and gave me an extra amount.

Al-Muwatta Chapter 31.43, 90: Malik said: "There is no harm in a person who has lent gold, silver, food or animals, taking something better than what was lent when that is not a stipulation between them nor a custom. If that is by a stipulation or promise or custom, then it is disapproved, and there is no good in it."

According to this principle, as a rule, if someone lends money or other resources to another person with a pre-condition of getting more than what is lent, it is not approved, but it is not explicitly disapproved either. In addition, it is not disapproved if the borrower while returning the borrowed amount, includes a gift or an additional amount.

Another way to reflect on this issue, in the light of the above *hadith* of the Prophet SAW, is that the answer to the above question of additional amount paid by the borrower depends upon the specific details. Given willingly, not resulting in any injustice, and resulting in some other benefit (legal or societal), in this case, goodwill, is not disapproved.

Can someone barter an amount of an item with another amount of the same or similar item?

There is a well-quoted incident in the *Hadith* literature when *Hazrat* Bilal, may Allah SWT be please with him, brought some dates of higher quality to the Prophet SAW, and the Prophet asked him about their origin. He stated that he bartered a larger amount of different types of dates with a smaller amount of these high-quality ones. The prophet got upset and disapproved the transaction. He stated that the right way to handle that transaction was to sell the first type of dates and use proceeds to

Chapter 12 – The Riba and Finance in the Hadith Literature

buy the second one. The following are relevant a*hadith* about this type of transaction:

> Sahih Al-Bukhari[2] Vol 3, 506: Narrated Abu Said al-Khudri RA: Once Bilal RA brought Barni (ie, a kind of dates) to the Prophet SAW and the Prophet asked him, "From where have you brought these?" Bilal replied, "I had some inferior type of dates and exchanged two Sa's of it for one Sa of Barni dates in order to give to the Prophet to eat." Thereupon the Prophet said, "Beware! Beware! This is definitely *Riba* (usury)! This is definitely *Riba* (usury)! Don't do so, but if you want to buy (a superior kind of dates) sell the inferior dates for money and then buy the superior kind of dates with that money."

> Sunan Abu Dawud, Vol. 4, 3348. It was narrated that 'Umar said: "The Messenger of Allah SAW said: 'Gold for silver is *Riba* unless exchanged on the spot; wheat for wheat is *Riba* unless exchanged on the spot; dates for dates is *Ribã* unless exchanged on the spot; and barley for barley is *Riba*, unless exchanged on the spot." *(Sahih)*

> Sunan Abu Dawud, Vol. 4, 3349: It was narrated from 'Ubãdah bin As-Samit that the Messenger of Allah SAW said: "Gold for gold, pure or minted; silver for silver, pure or minted; wheat for wheat with equal measure; barley for barley with equal measure; dates for dates with equal measure; salt for salt with equal measure. Whoever gives more or asks for more has engaged in *Riba*. There is nothing wrong with selling gold for silver hand to hand, if silver is more, but if it is on credit,

— 105

then no. And there is nothing wrong with selling wheat for barley hand to hand, if barley is more, but if it is on credit, then no." *(Sahih)*

Sahih Al-Bukhari2, Vol. 3, 294: The Prophet MPBUH said, "No (bartering of) two *Sa'a's* (of dates in this incident when someone bartered two *Sa'a's* of inferior dates with one *Sa'a* of better dates) for one *Sa'a*, or two Dirhams for one Dirham, is permissible."

One may ask, why someone may barter two Dirhams (or two dollars) for one Dirham (or a dollar)? There seems to be no logical or plausible reason for this type of transaction unless something else is also happening. One easy explanation is that this is about deferred payment, one Dirham of today with two on a later date, which is forbidden. The other example of this may be as follows: If one takes a very used and dirty dollar bill to someone (a bank or a trader) and the other party takes a position that they will not accept its face value and will only give 50 cents worth of material or change for it. This transaction is not permitted, because the person would lose from no fault of their own. I read about a similar ancient abusive practice inflicted upon poor people, the ones who had few resources and smaller denomination of the local currency, by the temple administration. Interestingly, I also noted the same practice in Pakistan when I tried to exchange US dollars with rupees. I was quoted lower rates per dollar for $20 bills in comparison to $100.

In terms of bartering dates of different qualities, there is an uncertainty of not exactly knowing the price and the market value of each variety, which may lead to either a financial loss for either party, or loss of trust between the trading parties. Using a standard of the marketplace and selling each good separately avoids or minimizes this problem. One can argue that one may barter these goods if both parties clearly understand the value of each merchandise at the time of transaction, including its details, especially of any fault if there is one, and barter in amounts based upon their respective market values.

The most important message from the above *ahadith* is about the fundamental nature and underpinning of *Riba*. In these examples, the issue is not of an additional amount, or the delay in payment (deferment), which implies that *Riba* is more than just an additional amount or interest, it is in fact about what is fair, and avoidance of unfairness, as the Quran conveys to us, no injustice to either party.

Can someone decide for a barter transaction to be done at a later time or date?

Hand-to-hand trade means bartering on the spot at the time of trade, when parties are physically present, as the situation may suddenly change as soon as the trading parties are separated. In modern day trading, this may apply to as long as they are in direct contact, physically, or digitally. Once the connection (a phone call or similar digital connection) is over, the situation is different. The following are some relevant a*hadith*:

> Sahih Al-Bukhari[2], Vol. 3, 344: The Prophet SAW said, "The bartering of gold for silver (some said gold for gold) is *Riba* except if it is from hand to hand, and wheat grain for wheat grain is *Riba* except if it is from hand to hand, and dates for

dates is *Riba* except if it is from hand to hand, and barley for barely is *Riba* except if it is from hand to hand."

Sahih Muslim Vol. 4, Chapter 15, [4066] 83 – (1588): It was narrated that Abu Hurairah said: "The Messenger of Allah SAW said: 'Dates for dates, wheat for wheat, barley for barley, salt for salt, like for like, hand to hand. Whoever gives more or asks for more, he has engaged in *Riba*, except in cases where the types differ.'"

Sahih Muslim Vol. 4, Chapter 10, [3857] 46 – (. . .) It was narrated from Abdullah bin Dinar that he heard Ibn Umar say: "The Messenger of Allah SAW said: 'There is no deal between two parties until they part, unless they choose to agree on a deal.'"

As described before, a transaction of like with like (wheat with wheat or salt with salt) does not make any sense unless something else is also happening, either a deferred transaction or an alternate hidden incentive for one party. These a*hadith*, the way they are recorded, do not provide any further clarification. One may say that it is about restricting exchange of similar items, except hand-to-hand. If this is the message of these a*hadith*, one may not borrow a ton of wheat to be returned sometime later, let's say a month later. But there seem not be any problem with that transaction (as per the understanding from Al-Muwatta), if no arrangement is made to have an additional amount added to what is borrowed. So, it cannot just be about exchange of similar items on a later date.

Alternatively, one can say that the issue is about the timing, and only hand-to-hand trade is allowed. But

Chapter 12 – The Riba and Finance in the Hadith Literature

as noted below, in the context of ordering agricultural products, arrangement of a trade to be completed on a future date is allowed. It cannot be that either.

The difference between trading on the spot, i.e., hand-to-hand, and with a lag of any amount of time period is that several factors may come into play and change the situation. First, the price of a commodity may change, which in today's fast-paced market system is a well-known concept. Trading prices for commodities may change from one second to another. So, trading a ton of wheat for a ton of wheat at future date can be inherently unfair to one of the parties. The recommended way is to buy a ton of wheat. One may say that this type of change in price may also happen while the parties are together (on the spot or hand-to-hand). That is true but it is a reasonable and fair compromise as both parties are free to access the market data and are free to walk away without a deal. Once they depart or the connection breaks, the deal is binding. If we compare these concepts to today's market system in the U.S.A., in some but not all situations, a similar concept is used except that usually there is a short duration of a day or a few days, after parties finalize the trade, during which the buyer may still cancel the trade. For example, this kind of relaxation or incentive is available while buying a television, but not for a stock purchase, which may be because the price of a television, compared to the price of a stock, is less likely to fluctuate and thus carries lesser risk of devaluation. This relaxation of a time period enjoyed by the buyer during which he or she may return the merchandise is also mentioned in Al-Muwatta, as practiced within the early Muslims of Madinah, with an understanding that the merchandise was returnable, or the price negotiable, if the item was found defective.

The Islamic Finance and the Riba

Despite the list of multiple commodities in these a*hadith*, it is intuitive that people normally have no interest in trading a ton of wheat with a ton of wheat, unless something else is going on. As far as trading one quality of wheat with a different quality of wheat is concerned, this issue was dealt with in a previous *hadith* with the example of trading different varieties of dates. What may have been prohibited is the bartering a ton of wheat of today with a ton of wheat in any future time or date, probably because of the uncertainties involved. As it is impossible to predict the exact monetary value of a ton of wheat in the future, this kind of deferred trade is likely unjust to one party. The preferred way is to buy the product at market price.

Some early Muslims, as described in Al-Muwatta, understood the messages in these a*hadith* in another manner, an understanding partly based upon an incident when the Prophet SAW asked someone to go and sell in the market an item made of either silver or gold. Exact details are murky, but the main lesson learned by some was that the item could not be sold for more than the exact weight of the metal it was made of. If we accept that understanding as valid, one may not charge anything extra for the labor of making a gold or silver utensil, or a piece of jewelry, or a machine part. If applied broadly, one may not charge extra for a shirt made of cotton, more than what the base price of raw cotton may be, a counter intuitive notion. To deal with this problem, it was suggested that the above rule only applied when trading gold, silver, or food. An understanding, which results in a different set of problems, about the basis and applicability of what is understood as *Riba*. My purpose of quoting this example here is that it is better for us to review and understand the basic rules of Islamic

Chapter 12 – The Riba and Finance in the Hadith Literature

Finance and the *Riba* and apply them to the products and examples of our time, instead of using the examples of how early people may have handled them.

Can someone pay in advance for a crop to be delivered on a later date?

Apparently, this was a common practice in Madinah, before the Prophet SAW arrived there, and during his later life. The related contract or arrangement was usually for 1-3 years. It was understood that this kind of arrangement of deferred payment, despite uncertainties involved, was valid in some situations. This was probably due to the requirements (in this case, agriculture) of arranging labor, seeds, months to years of work, and its benefit to the larger society (example of cost-benefit analysis). The following are the relevant a*hadith:*

> Sahih Al-Bukhari[2], Vol 3, 441: Narrated Ibn Abbas, RA Allah's Apostle SAW came to Medina and the people used to pay in advance the price of fruits to be delivered within one or two years (the sub-narrator is in doubt whether it was one to two years or two to three years.) The Prophet SAW said, "Whoever pays money in advance for dates (to be delivered later) should pay it for known specified weight and measure (of the dates)."

> Sahih Muslim Vol. 4, Chapter 25, [4118] 127 – (1604): It was narrated that Ibn Abbas said: "When the Prophet SAW came to Al-Madinah, they used to pay one to two years in advance for fruits. He said: 'Whoever pays for fruits in advance, let him pay in advance for a specified measure and a specified weight, for a specified amount of time.'"

Sahih Al-Bukhari[2], Vol 3, 446: Narrated Shuba: Muhammad or Abdullah bin Abu Al-Mujalid said, "Abdullah bin Shaddad and Abu Burda differed regarding As-Salam, so they sent me to ibn Abi Aufa RA and I asked him about it. He replied, 'In the life-time of Allah's Apostle SAW, Abu Bakr and Umar, we used to pay in advance the prices of wheat, barley, dried grapes and dates to be delivered later. I also asked Ibn Abza and he, too, replied as above."

Permission of paying in advance for delivery of the bought product on a later date was not automatically allowed in every situation, different situations were dealt differently. For example:

Sahih Al-Bukhari[2], Vol 3, 451: Narrated Abu Bakhtari At-Tai: I asked Ibn Abbas RA about Salam for (the fruits of) date palms. He replied, The Prophet SAW forbade the sale of dates on the trees till their benefit becomes evident and till they are fit for eating and also the sale of silver (for gold) on credit." I asked Ibn Abbas about Salam for dates and he replied, "The Prophet SAW forbade the sale of dates till they were fit for eating and could be estimated."

This *hadith*, at least partly, seems to contradict the previous two *ahadith*, which allowed paying in advance for a crop to be delivered later. The first two *ahadith* were about an ongoing practice in the community. The message was that one can arrange with a farmer for a certain amount of crop to be delivered sometime during a pre-agreed time frame (e.g., 1-3 years), with its price paid or arranged in advance. The third *hadith* was about a particular local practice of paying for the unpicked fruit on the tree. The buyer was not just paying for a certain amount of dates to be delivered later, which could be a valid transaction, instead, the buyer was making a deal while the dates on a particular tree or trees had not ripened yet. In this arrangement, there were two problems: a. A pest or blight might destroy a part of the dates after the payment was made and the discovery was made later at harvest time, b. The amount of fruit could only be guessed instead of making an exact measurement. Waiting until the fruit was ready to be picked, if the trading parties were trying for a fair and doubt-free deal, benefited both the buyer and the seller. It helped to avoid any potential conflict arising from unforeseen circumstances, i.e., it helped to avoid the *dharar* and the *gharar* (discussed underneath). The following *ahadith* provide grounds for this explanation:

> Sahih Muslim Vol 4, Chapter 4, [3991] 18 – (1556): It was narrated that Abu Saeed Al Khudri said: "At the time of the Messenger of Allah SAW, a man suffered loss of some fruit that he had bought, and his debts mounted. The Messenger of Allah said: 'Give him charity,' and the people gave him charity, but it was not enough to pay off his debt. The Messenger of Allah said to his creditors: 'Take what you find, and you are not entitled to any more than that.'"

> Sunan Abu Dawud, Vol. 4, 3367: It was narrated from Abdullah bin Umar that the Messenger of Allah SAW forbade selling fruits before they are ripe; he forbade that for the seller and the buyer as well. (Sahih)

Sunan Abu Dawud, Vol. 4, 3368: It was narrated from Ibn Umar that the Messenger of Allah SAW forbade selling palm trees until they ripened, and ears of grain until they turned white and were free of blight; he forbade that for the seller and the buyer as well. (Sahih)

Sunan Abu Dawud, Vol. 4, 3372: Yunus said: "I asked Abu Az-Zinad about selling crops before they are ripe and what was said about that. He said: "Urwah bin Az-Zubair narrated from Sahl bin Abi Hatmah, that Zaid bin Thabit said: "The people used to sell crops before they were ripe, then when the people harvested the crop and payment was demanded, the buyer would say: "It has been stricken with *Duman*, or *Qusham* or *Murad* – types of blight concerning which they disputed. When many disputes were referred to the Prophet SAW, the Messenger of Allah SAW said, as if offering advice: 'No, do not sell crops until they have ripened" because there were too many disputes and differences among them." (Sahih)

Sahih Muslim Vol. 4, Chapter 13, [3865] 51 – (1534): It was narrated that Ibn Umar said: "The Messenger of Allah SAW said: 'Do not sell produce until its goodness appears and there is no longer fear of blight.'"

It is important to mention that despite the prohibition of the type of sale based upon conjecture, as described above, in some situations the Prophet SAW did allow it. For example:

Sunan Abu Dawud, Vol. 4, 3363: It was narrated

from Sahl bin Abi Hatmah that the Messenger of Allah SAW forbade selling fresh dates for dry dates, but he granted a concession in the case of 'Araya' allowing them to be sold by estimate, so that its owners (who bought it) could eat fresh dates. (Sahih).

Sunan Abu Dawud, Vol. 4, 3365: It was narrated from Abd Rabbih bin Saeed Al-Ansari that he said: "Araya means that a man lends a palm tree to another man (to benefit from its harvest) or he sells the yield of a few specific trees to another man in exchange for dried dates." (Sahih)

The explanation provided in the commentary of the *hadith*, about *araya* sale, was that it was done for a larger benefit or to avoid a different kind of problem. As a result, one of the messages obtained from these examples is that the situation matters, and rules might be bent for a larger benefit or to avoid a larger problem. Yet another explanation is that there is no bending of rules. Instead, in these seemingly contradictory situations a unique but uniform rule is followed, which seems hidden or is not so obvious. I shall continue this discussion later in this writing.

What about the transactions involving ambiguity?

Sunan Abu Dawud Vol. 4, 3376: It was narrated from Abu Hurairah that the Prophet SAW forbade transactions involving ambiguity. "Uthman (one of the narrators) added: "and *Al-Hasah*."

Gharar or ambiguity can be of multiple types, e.g., lack of clarity of timing, quantity, the type of product, etc. Multiple *ahadith* are available, which indirectly address this issue but, probably due to its significance, in the above *hadith* the Prophet SAW addressed it directly and specifically. The classic example quoted in the *Hadith* was about the sale of an unborn animal. This was about another custom of that time in Arabia when people paid in advance for the offspring, or the offspring of an offspring, of a camel. This kind of sale was ambiguous as it carried the risk that the offspring might not be born, or might be stillborn, or might not be normal. Waiting until the birth and examining the animal before the trade minimized the risk. Aside from its direct implication which might be limited in today's world, this, the previous, and the following a*hadith* provided an important principle that was used by jurists for analogical analysis, the concept of ambiguity or *gharar* (to be discussed in detail later) in financial transactions.

> Sahih Al-Bukhari[2], Vol 3, 457: Narrated Abdullah RA: The people used to sell camels on the basis of *Habal-al-Habala*. The Prophet SAW forbade such sale. Nafi explained *Habal-al-Habala* by saying. "The camel is to be delivered to the buyer after the she-camel gives birth."

Habal-al-Habala sale also involved paying for an unborn child of a she-camel.

Is money exchange allowed in Islam?

> Sahih Al-Bukhari[3] Vol. 3, Chapter 34, 2060, 2061: Narrated Abu Al-Minhal: I used to practice money exchange, and I asked Zaid bin Arqam RA about it, and he narrated what the Prophet SAW

said (as follows): Abu Al-Minhal said, "I asked Al-Bar bin Azib and Zaid bin Arqam about practicing money exchange. They replied, 'We were traders in the lifetime of Allah's Messenger SAW and I asked Allah's Messenger SAW about money exchange. He replied, "If it is from hand to hand, there is no harm in it; but if there is *Nasia* (delay in payment) then it is not permissible."'

As the value of every currency may fluctuate rather quickly, delayed or deferred payment for money exchange can easily be inherently unjust for one party, and not allowed. Only hand to hand or spot money exchange is allowed.

What about people who facilitate a *Riba* transaction?

In a *Riba* based system, many people can be involved, other than a borrower and a lender. There can be someone deputizing the transaction (e.g., an attorney), someone documenting it, and others witnessing it. The following *ahadith* addressed different parts of this system:

> Sahih Muslim Vol. 4, Chapter 19, [4092] 105 – (1597): It was narrated that Abdullah said: "The Messenger of Allah SAW cursed the one who consumes *Riba* **and the one who pays it.**" I (the narrator) said: "And the one who writes it down and the two who witness it?" He said: "We only narrate what we heard."

> Sahih Muslim Vol. 4, Chapter 19, [4093] 106 – (1598): It was narrated that Jabir said: "The Messenger of Allah SAW cursed the one who

consumes *Riba* and **the one who pays it**, the one who writes it down and the two who witness it," and he said: "They are all the same."

Sunan Abu Dawud, Vol. 4, Chapter 4, 3333: 'AbdurRehman bin Abdullah bin Masud narrated that his father said: "The Messenger of Allah SAW cursed the one who consumes *Riba*, the one who pays it, the one who witnesses it and the one who records it." (Hasan)

Most of what is stated in these *ahadith* is without disagreement, except the issue of 'the one who pays it'. The confusion is about the part of the *ahadith* where the words '*aakil*' and '*mwakkal*' are used.

The word *mwakkal* results in confusion, as one may finds its two different spellings. This results in lack of clarity about its root word. Most people understand it as a derivative of *aakil (alif, kaaf,* and *laam)*, but some disagree and consider it a derivative of *wakkal (wao, kaaf,* and *laam)*. If it was derived from the root word *aakil*, it meant 'the one who feeds' but if it was from *wakkal*, the translation was 'the one who deputizes'. Other than its correct root, or spelling, there are other linguistic factors to consider. For example, words are understood based upon their context, their proverbial usage, and technical meanings. And sometimes there are other matters to consider, such as the nature of the message being conveyed, especially its significance in the overall scheme of things.

In spite of all that, one group believes that the root *aakil* for this word makes more sense in these *ahadith* but others disagree, suggesting that *wakkal i*s more appropriate.

Chapter 12 – The Riba and Finance in the Hadith Literature

Reading most translations that I could find; I noted that the first group prevailed more than the second. But is that the correct position to take and is there a problem accepting one position over the other?

Before any further discussion, it is important to point out that irrespective of what one may understand about this word in these a*hadith*, it will not change any injunctions against *Riba*. The Quran is clear about outlawing *Riba*, and the terrible fate waiting for the ones consuming it, in this world and the hereafter. But the Quranic message is also accommodating and merciful for the ones forced to pay it.

The Quran, Al-Baqarah, *ayat* 278-281 (Al-Quran 2:278-280)

> "O ye who believe! Fear Allah, and give up what remains of your demand for usury, if ye are indeed believers. If ye do it not, take notice of war from Allah and His Messenger: But if ye turn back, ye shall have your capital sums; deal not unjustly, and ye shall not be dealt with unjustly. If the debtor is in a difficulty, grant him time till it is easy for him to repay. But if ye remit it by way of charity, that is best for you if ye only knew." Ali.

> "O you who believe! Be afraid of Allah and give up what remains (due to you) from *Riba* (usury) (from now onward), if you are (really) believers. And if you do not do it, then take a notice of war from Allah and His messenger, but if you repent, you shall have your capital sums. Deal not unjustly (by asking more than your capital sums), and you shall not be dealt with unjustly

(by receiving less than your capital sums. And if the debtor is in a hard time (has no money), then grant him time till it is easy for him to repay, but if you remit it by way of charity, that is better for you if you did but know." Al-Hilali & Khan.

For the *ahadith* described above, accepting the first version, 'the one who feeds' instead of 'the one who deputizes' (*aakil* instead of *wakaal*) results in two problems: a. The Quranic message, or injunction, or recommendation about the debtor (the one who is paying *Riba*) is very merciful. Putting him or her in the same category with one, who consumes, deputizes, witnesses or records a *Riba* transaction, results in a type of internal inconsistency between the message of the Quran and the *Hadith*, and b. If an Islamic system ever tries to outlaw and penalize the practice of *Riba*, it will also have to punish the one borrowing the money, which does not make sense.

Is it allowed to ask for collateral for a credit sale?

> Sahih Muslim Vol. 4, Chapter 24, [4114] 124 – (1603): It was narrated that Aishah said: "The Messenger of Allah SAW bought some food on credit from a Jew, and he gave him a coat of mail of his as collateral."

Asking for a collateral carrying some monetary value is allowed. An abuse of this option is to demand an illegal and unethical collateral. In historically abusive societies, a lender kept the borrowers or his family's physical service (labor) as collateral, if the debt with or without usury was not fully paid. In the worst-case scenario, the debtor or his family member, such as a child was enslaved. In contrast to these negative examples, in the USA, in commercial or business lending situations, a debtor's primary home or automobile cannot not be used, during his or her lifetime, to pay off the debt.

Can someone borrow more than what he/she can pay off?

Borrowing is allowed in Islam but with some strict guidelines. Not able to pay off debt is quite a serious matter, as mentioned in the following *ahadith:*

> Sunan Abu-Dawud Vol. 4, 3343: It was narrated that Jabir said: "The Messenger of Allah SWT would not offer the funeral prayer for a man who had died in debt. A deceased person was brought to him and he said: 'Does he owe any debt?' They said: 'Yes, two Dinars.' He said: "Offer the funeral prayer for your companion.' Abu Qatadah Al-Ansari said: 'I will pay them, O Messenger of Allah.' So the Messenger of Allah offered the funeral prayer for him. When Allah granted conquests to His Messenger, he said: 'I am more worthy of every believer than himself. Whoever leaves behind a debt, then refer it to me, and whoever leaves behind wealth, it is for his heirs.'"

As per this principle, a Muslim must be very careful not to borrow an amount that his or her estate may not be able to pay off, in case of a disease, disability or death. If that happens, it is better if his or her family or even friend(s) pay that amount to the lender. Even better, for the lender, is if he or she writes it off, as a charity.

CHAPTER 13

RIBA IN ISLAM – ITS BASIS AND NATURE

As described above *Riba* is prohibited in all three Abrahamic religions – Judaism, Christianity, and Islam. In comparison with the previous scriptures, the Islamic perspective on *Riba* is somewhat elaborate and expansive. Despite its clear prohibition, none of the sacred books (Jewish or Christian scriptures, the Quran, or the *Hadith*) provide a clear or unequivocal definition of all that *Riba* can be.

It seems, at least to a certain level, the concept of *Riba* for the early generations was a self-explanatory concept. For example, there was no documentation of a specific *hadith* or an account in the life history of the Prophet SAW, where someone specifically reported or inquired of him about *Riba's* definition, or any account where he narrated its comprehensive definition. *Ahadith* about *Riba* provided examples when, after having witnessed certain transactions, the Prophet provided his corrective or clarifying opinion. Despite its overt understanding as mentioned above, the lack of full clarity about the scope and implications of *Riba* was likely the reason that many people tried to provide their own explanations.

One may find an initial attempt to elaborate *Riba* in Al-Muwatta of Imam Malik (may Allah SWT be pleased with him) where a narration of Zayd ibn Aslam (may Allah SWT be pleased with him) is quoted, "Usury in the *jahiliyya* was that a man would give a loan to a man for a set term. When the term was due, he would say, 'Will you pay it off or increase me?' If the man paid, he took it. If not, he increased him in his debt and lengthened the term for him." This concept of *Riba* seems like what one may indirectly find in the Jewish, the Christian, and the pre-Islamic Arab traditions. On the other hand, for a Muslim, a review of some of the *ahadith* provides a somewhat expansive view of *Riba*. It is important to note that the inclusion of the above narration in Al-Muwatta clearly suggests that there was a need even early on for someone to define *Riba* in more clear terms.

Before going into the fundamentals of *Riba*, let's look at some attempts at its contemporary definitions. One common contemporary definition of *Riba* is that, in comparison to any legal profit, it is a religiously illegal 'increase', 'gain' or 'growth' from a financial or business transaction. But then the issue remains, religiously speaking, what is the religiously legal or illegal (forbidden) gain or growth or increase? Islam does not provide any detail about the extent of gain or growth, except stating that the transaction has to be Riba free, or just. According to another definition, using financial jargon, *Riba* is trading completely in credit. More commonly, people use a simpler or seemingly easier description of

Riba, with little further explanation, by stating that it is what Allah SWT does not allow. Probably, the most common practical understanding of *Riba* is that it is the 'interest' banks charge on a loan. What exactly is *Riba*? What may be the underlying principles defining a *Riba* transaction? Answering these questions can help to address the fundamental reasons about its prohibitions. In this section, I have tried to address these questions.

Were their different types of *Riba*?

For sake of understanding, some scholars have divided *Riba* in two types, but, a**s** I alluded above, if we understand the underlying principles for its prohibitions, this division seems arbitrary.

Type A:
Growth Through Deferment (delaying or postponing):
Al-Muwatta1 Chapter 31(39), 83: Malik related to me that Zayd bin Aslam said, "Usury in *Jahiliyya* was that a man would give a loan to a man for a set term. When the term was due, he would say, 'Will you pay it off or increase me?' If the man paid he took it. If not, he increased him in his debt and lengthened the term for him."

This is when the repayment of a loan is delayed while adding an amount to the principal (especially an unreasonable amount [Al-Qur'an 3:130]), if the loan is not paid off at the predetermined date. A good contemporary example is a credit card transaction which is an unrestricted loan or credit. If one does not pay the amount when it is due, the card company gives more time and makes the person pay an additional amount (most of the time, this amount or the rate charged is exuberant), which (the additional amount), if the full amount is not paid soon enough, can become quite large as more and more time is added – this is growth for the company through deferment and is considered the "forbidden" growth or the *Riba*.

Type B:
Growth Through Surplus:
Sahih Al-Bukhari2, Vol. 3, 294: Narrated Abu Said RA: We used to be given mixed dates (from the booty) and used to sell (barter) two Sa's (of those dates) for one Sa (of good dates). The Prophet SAW said (to us), "No (bartering) of two Sa's for one Sa, or two Dirhams for one Dirham is permissible."

This is the expected increase or additional amount, while exchanging fungible items, which, unlike what is stated above, is not necessarily time dependent. The expected additional amount is not because one party kept the borrowed material for a certain time period but rather for some other reason. The reason can be a hidden issue or a deception, or a possibility of either, in both delayed and on-the-spot or hand-to-hand transactions.
Let's look at the concept of fungibility first: Fungible items are interchangeable, like a dollar note with another dollar note, an ounce of gold with another ounce of gold, or a ton of wheat with another ton of wheat of the same kind. Non-fungible items are not inter-changeable, and every unit is relatively unique, like diamond or cattle, or an apartment. They can also have a different price based upon multiple factors. Typically, a fungible item or its value is measured in numbers or in weight e.g., money in numbers, and gold or grain in weight. The value of a non-fungible item is unique to each individual item and is not measured in this manner. It is also important to mention that a difference of opinion existed within

scholars about what items might qualify as fungible, some limiting it to exactly what was mentioned in one *hadith*: Sahih Al-Bukhari[2], Vol. 3, 344; while others relied on the general concept of fungibility, and extended its application to all items with the same qualities, using a different *hadith:* Sahih Muslim Vol. 4, [4063].

Sahih Al-Bukhari[2], Vol. 3, 344: Narrated by Umar bin Al-Khattab RA, Allah's Apostle SAW said, "The bartering of gold for silver (some said 'gold for gold') is Riba (usury) except if it is from hand to hand and wheat grain for wheat grain is usury except if it is from hand to hand, and dates for dates is usury except if it is from hand to hand, and barley for barley is usury except if it is from hand to hand."

Or the other:

Sahih Muslim, Vol. 4, [4063]: It was narrated that 'Ubadah bin As-Samit said: "The Messenger of Allah SAW said: "Gold for gold, silver for silver, wheat for wheat, barley for barley, dates for dates, salt for salt, like for like, same for same, hand to hand. But if these commodities differ, then sell as you like, as long as it is hand to hand."

Let's say someone borrows (as a business transaction) $1,000, or an ounce of gold or silver or a ton of wheat, to be returned or exchanged within the same time frame or on a later date, in either the same amount or more than what is originally borrowed. In both cases there can be a problem: in the first case (if the amount does not change and the transaction happened within the same timeframe – hand to hand) there is no justification for such an exchange unless there is some hidden agenda. If the same amount is returned after a time period, it can be unfair to one party due to any change in its price, and if an additional amount is demanded, it can still be unfair due to unpredictability of future prices, unless that issue is dealt with in some manner. The borrowing for business must be done in a way to keep it fair for both the borrower and the lender, with as little unpredictability as possible.

While trading in the same fungible item, the usual tendency is to trade one type with the other, like trading an inferior quality of wheat with a better quality of wheat, or one karat of gold with a different karat of gold, but these types of transactions are generally disapproved and are considered *Riba* transactions. Instead of bartering similar commodities, the recommendation by the Prophet SAW was to sell one item as per market rate and buy the other with the proceeds. It is possible that all that can be achieved at the time of making a business deal on the spot, hand-to-hand, if both parties are free and able to figure out the monetary value of each other's products. The likely logic of disapproval with same item bartering, without an intermediary step of sale and purchase, is to safeguard against any misunderstanding or conflict arising due to uncertainties about either the merchandise or the market conditions.

During the early part of Islamic civilization, gold and silver were available in minted or un-minted forms. Apparently, coins in those days were not minted in Arabia, which, as per information on the net, started in 70s AH. It was likely that the market value of minted gold or silver was different from their un-minted forms and was dealt differently. Even today, one cannot say that all form of gold or silver is same and fungible (interchangeable). A precious piece of jewelry made from

Chapter 13 – Riba in Islam Its Basis and Nature

gold or silver may carry significantly more value than its raw metallic form. Jewelers in Pakistan, while providing detail pricing of their products, routinely separate the price of gold (by weight), and the cost of making the jewelry. To make the right decision, every situation requires consideration of all such pertinent factors.

In a different manner, there is no justification, within the same time frame or hand to hand, to trade $1,000 with $1,000, or with $1,000 + any additional amount. If a similar transaction is happening with a lag of a certain time period, it is still not permitted. This is because if the same amount is returned, one party may lose due to change in market conditions, and if a pre-set additional amount (without any standard or control) is returned, one party may still lose due to the impossibility of figuring out exact value of an item on a future date or in a future time period. To safeguard the interests of both parties in a business transaction and to minimize uncertainty (which may lead to either fraud, conflict or a lack of trust), Islam recommends an alternate approach to this conventional way of doing business. Without a description of what that approach might be, it recommends an approach that does not involve *Riba*. We are free to devise any such *Riba*-free business plan. Borrowing for a personal matter is a somewhat different subject, but the rules of *Riba* are not any different and still applicable.

It was important to understand that the division of *Riba* in types, as described above, is arbitrarily done, for our better understanding. It is also clear that most of the time when people talked about *Riba*, they talk about its first type. This is because it is relatively easy to understand in that manner, with ancient historical context. The Islamic concept of *Riba*, on the other hand, is much more complex, and to understand it properly one must understand its so-called both types. One can, in fact, argue that the basic or underlying reasons for its prohibition are the same or similar for both or all types of *Riba*. To fully grasp its significance and intricacies, one requires a thorough understanding of the reasons and principles behind *Riba*.

Going Deeper to Find Underlying Principles of *Riba*

There are two ways to address the issue of the underlying principles of *Riba*. Many may say that we shall stick with what is already understood, based upon the Quran and the *Sunnah*, or by the early generations of Muslims, and avoid further discussion. According to this position, there may not be a need for any further or analogical reasoning. One may accept this position provided there was no difference of opinion within early generations of Muslims about this matter. Secondly, even if one takes a position that no further discussion or exploration of fundamental reasoning behind all types of *Riba* is needed, one cannot solve many problems.

By taking the conservative position of no further discussion or analogical reasoning, we must then accept that the *Riba* rules may not apply to many modern-day transactions and business arrangements and shall apply only in situations described in the *Hadith*. I am reasonably certain that people who may take the conservative position will likely not agree with this notion either. But we cannot have it both ways, either we accept the conservative position and not consider *Riba* for many modern-day transactions, the type not mentioned in the *Hadith*, or alternatively not accept the conservative position and find the underlying rules that can be applied

Chapter 13 – Riba in Islam Its Basis and Nature

to any financial arrangement of any time. In fact, the logical way out is to accept the latter position and find the underlying principles behind the concept of *Riba*. Once deciphered, these rules or principles may be used to make decisions about present day finance.

In an efficient system of governance, rules are not made to tell people how to live their life or how to do business, they are designed to prevent damage or harm from one person to the other, to property, or to society. Similarly, in Islamic finance rules are not meant to dictate people how to do their business or make business decisions, but rather to define what to avoid. Also, these rules, our understanding of their basis, their utility, and their application must be internally consistent, i.e., consistent within each other and with the general Islamic principles. For example, a business arrangement can never be 'Islamic', even if there is no *Riba* involved, if it is, for any other reason, unjust or exploitative to one party, as Islam does not accept injustice or exploitation. It is also important to mention that something that was clearly prohibited by Allah SWT in His Book or by His Prophet SAW is forbidden, even if it does not involve *Riba*, or if its logic seem debatable.

The instructions about *Riba*, or the *ayat* making it categorically illegal is considered a part of the last revelation to the Prophet SAW. Soon after, he passed away and Muslims lost the luxury of his un-contestable clarifying authority on this subject. It is a common understanding that, despite its clear prohibition, there was at least some confusion about its nature. In my opinion, the Quran, with its signature style, like putting a (proverbial) river in a water-sac, clearly describes the fundamental nature of *Riba*. Right after the injunction about its prohibition, it states: (The Quran, Al Baqarah, 279 [Al-Quran 2:279]) " . . . deal not unjustly and ye shall not be dealt with unjustly." In a way, informing us that the *Riba* fundamentally is an act of injustice of financial type, which is not allowed in Islam.

Not only that any act of injustice is prohibited, any action that may lead to it is also not allowed. This understanding is especially helpful to appreciate the logic of *Riba* in some situations, where there is no deferment, and no additional amount or usury involved. Though the *ayat* of the Quran about *Riba* were part of the last revelations, and some level of uncertainty about *Riba* existed even in the first generation of Muslims, there *were* numerous *ahadith* of the Prophet SAW about this subject. But the information available to us in the *Hadith* literature is understandable only if we comprehend the fundamental principle of *Riba*, instead of calling it "interest" or usury, or even an additional amount on a loan. The Quran provides its fundamental principle, but it is the *Hadith* literature that provides us expansive practical detail of that principle, if not its explicit definition. Without the input from the *Hadith*, our understanding of *Riba* cannot be complete, and can easily be misleading.

For the Muslim community, the declaration of the injunction about *Riba* was made by the Prophet SAW when he delivered his famous speech in Arafat. In the speech, he specifically forbade or ended certain customs or traditions of the Days of Ignorance, the time of the *"Jahiliyya"*, for the early Muslims. He specifically forbade the *Riba* of *Jahiliyya*. But, in the speech he did not provide a proper definition or its fundamental basis. Reading and analyzing the *Hadith* literature, we see that the Muslim community at times struggled with this concept, and the Prophet SAW provided his corrective advice. In the *Hadith* literature, we find a reference in the Al-Muwatta about the *Riba* of *Jahiliyya*, providing us some insight about how that generation understood this subject. As per this description, *Riba* of *Jahiliyya* was the historically abusive money-lending practice. But that was just one of its aspects, much more detail about *Riba* can be found in the *Hadith* literature. Reviewing all that information provide us a much larger or expansive concept of *Riba*. As I stated above, after the Quran, probably the most important *hadith* of the Prophet SAW about this subject is as follows:

> Sahih Al-Bukhari[2] Vol 3, 506: Narrated Abu Said al-Khudri RA: Once Bilal RA brought Barni (ie, a kind of dates) to the Prophet SAW and the Prophet asked him, "From where have you brought these?" Bilal replied, "I had some inferior type of dates and exchanged two Sa's of it for one Sa of Barni dates in order to give to the Prophet to eat." Thereupon the Prophet said, "Beware! Beware! This is definitely *Riba* (usury)! This is definitely *Riba* (usury)! Don't do so, but if you want to buy (a superior kind of dates) sell the inferior dates for money and then buy the superior kind of dates with that money."

We do not have any more information in reference to any conversation between the Prophet SAW and Bilal RA, where he might have asked the Prophet SAW for explanation. Reviewing this narration in addition to many other *ahadith* provides us insight into the underlying problem with the way Bilal RA conducted this transaction vs what the Prophet SAW recommended.

To understand the underlying problem, or the *Riba* in this transaction as the Prophet SAW mentioned, we must understand two concepts described by scholars, as the *Dharar*, and the *Gharar* in the context of a financial transaction.

Dharar, in a financial transaction, means avoidable or unjustifiable financial harm (or loss) by one party to the other. If a product is sold in the open market by every other trader at $5 a pound, and one trader (may be outside the marketplace) is selling the same product at $7 a pound, the extra charge of $2 is *dharar*. It can easily be avoided by following the market or the market-standards. The concept of *dharar* is not explicitly mentioned in the Quran and is rather derived from relevant general principles of not inflicting any harm, and similarly from the *Hadith*. Its multiple variations, based upon the subject and the context involved, can be found in different *ayat* of the Quran. For example:

The Quran, Al-Baqarah, *ayah* 295 (Al-Quran 2:195)
"And spend of your substance in the cause of Allah, and make not your own hands contribute to (your) destruction; but do good; for Allah loveth those who do good." Ali.
"And spend in the Cause of Allah (i.e. *Jihad* of all kinds etc.) and do not throw yourselves into destruction (by not spending your wealth in the Cause of Allah), and do good. Truly, Allah loves *Al-Muhsinun* (the good-doers)." Al-Hilali &Khan.

The Quran, Al-Baqarah, *ayah* 231 (Al-Quran 2:231)
"When ye divorce women, and they are about to fulfill the term of their *('Iddah)*, either retain them or let them go; but do not retain them to

injure them, (or) to take undue advantage; if anyone does that, he wrongs his own soul. Do not treat Allah's Signs as a jest, but solemnly rehearse Allah's favours on you, and that fact that He sent down to you the Book and Wisdom, for your instruction. And fear Allah, and know that Allah is well-acquainted with all things." Ali.

"And when you have divorced women and they have fulfilled the term of their prescribed period, either take them back on reasonable basis or set them free on reasonable basis. But do not take them back to hurt them, and whoever does that, then he has wronged himself. And treat not the Verses (Laws) of Allah as a jest, but remember Allah's Favours on you (i.e. Islam), and that which He has sent down to you of the Book (i.e. the Qur'an) and *Al-Hikmah* (the Prophet's *Sunnah* – legal ways – Islamic jurisprudence etc.) whereby He instructs you. And fear Allah, and know that Allah is All-Aware of everything." Al-Hilali and Khan.

There is also a *hadith* of the Prophet SAW on this subject: Sunan ibn Majah, Vol. 3, 2340: "There should be neither harming nor reciprocating harm."

The term *dharar* meant harm or damage or loss to one party by the other, or at the cost of one to the other. The root word is *dhar*, with meanings of injury, harm, loss, deprivation, etc. (in physical, psychological, financial or even in spiritual aspects). In financial terms, it implies a loss or disadvantage inflicted upon one party by the other, by design or deceit, instead of due to market or natural conditions. For example, in gambling, it is certain that one party will lose. Ideally, there should not be any harm to either party from a financial transaction, or if there is risk of harm or loss, somehow it should be equal for all parties. Any amount of *dharar* without valid legal justification is injustice, which, as outlined above, is not allowed.

Gharar, in a financial transaction, means avoidable or unjustifiable financial uncertainty or deception. If the same trader in the above example is justifying the higher price with claims that are either doubtful, misleading, or false, he is dealing with *gharar*. The term of *Riba*, as understood by the Quran and the *Hadith* literature, is a part of a financial transaction or a contract, which has either *dharar*, or *gharar*, or both. For a financial transaction to be *Riba*-free, both *dharar* and *gharar* must be either eliminated or minimized. *Riba* is a sin, and just like any other sin, it may be difficult to eliminate it from a society, but every effort should be made to minimize it.

In the example of the *hadith* above, the Prophet SAW recommended Bilal RA to sell one type of dates, preferably in the market where he would have full access to its market-value at the time of sale and buy the second kind of dates in the same manner. Doing it in this manner minimized *dharar*: any chances of financial harm or loss to Bilal RA or the other party. In addition, it avoided *gharar*: any possible misunderstanding, guilt, or feeling of being cheated (if the market price of one type of dates was different from what Bilal RA or the other party had stipulated). Elimination or minimization of *dharar* and *gharar* fulfilled the Quranic instructions about the *Riba, la tazlaymoona wa la tuzlamoon*, no injustice to either or any party. Both *dharar* and *gharar* in financial transactions or contracts can take a variety of forms, thus explaining the statement of the Prophet SAW that there can be "73" or way too many types or levels of *Riba*.

When talking about justice in any system, it is imperative to know the rights from wrongs. In the following chapter, I discuss some general rules of finance, which help to figure out what is right and wrong, or what is just or not as per Islamic principles or its traditions.

CHAPTER 14

THE RULES OF ISLAMIC FINANCE

In this chapter an effort is made to formulate and describe basic rules of Islamic finance. Before one may review the principles underlying Islamic finance, or the *Riba*, or for that matter any aspect of our lives, it is important to declare and establish appropriate source standards. For our subject matter, the criterion for what is right or allowed, and what is wrong or prohibited, is derived from the Quran:

The Quran, Al-Imran, *ayah* 4 (Al-Quran 3:4)

> "It is He Who sent down to thee (step by step), in truth, the Book, confirming what went before it; and He sent down the Law (of Moses) and the Gospel (of Jesus) before this, as a guide to mankind, and He sent down the Criterion (of judgment between right and wrong) . . . " Ali.

> "It is He Who has sent down the Book (the Qur'an) to you (Muhammad SAW) with truth, confirming what came before it. And he sent down the Taurat (Torah) and the Injeel (Gospel). Aforetime, as a guidance to mankind, and He sent down the criterion (of judgment between right and wrong [this Quran]) . . . " Al-Hilali & Khan.

This criterion includes an important rule: we are required to obey Allah SWT's commands but also His Prophet Muhammad SAW:

The Quran, Al-Imran, *ayah* 32 (Al-Quran 3:32)

> "Say: "Obey Allah and His Messenger": But if they turn back, Allah liveth not those who reject Faith." Ali.

> "Say (O Muhammad SAW): "Obey Allah and the Messenger (Muhammad SAW)." But if they turn away, then Allah does not like the disbelievers." Al-Hilali & Khan.

Guidance is obtained from the Quran but also from the Prophet Muhammad SAW, as the Quran does not address many practical details. After the Prophet SAW passed away, the guidance from him was in the form of his documented biography, his statements, and his actions. We are asked to follow this principle, of obtaining guidance from the Quran and the Prophet SAW, with a warning:

The Quran, Al-Nisa, *ayah* 14 (Al-Quran 4:14)

> "But those who disobey Allah and His Messenger and transgress His limits will be admitted to

a Fire, to abide therein: And they shall have a humiliating punishment." Ali.

"And whosoever disobeys Allah and His Messenger (Muhammad SAW), and transgresses His limits, He will cast him into the Fire, to abide therein; and he shall have a disgraceful torment." Al-Hilali & Khan.

To make it even more clear, and describing the rule in practical and explicit terms, Allah SWT mentions in the Quran:

The Quran, Al-Hashar, *ayah* 7 (Al-Quran 59:7).

"… So take what the Messenger assigns to you, and deny yourselves that which he withholds from you…". Ali.

"… And whatsoever the Messenger (Muhammad SAW) gives you, take it, and whatsoever he forbids you, abstain (from it)…". Al-Hilali & Khan.

As far as the traditional conflict about what *Hadith* literature to accept or not accept, as I stated above, many scholars have enshrined certain impressions or opinions within their religious understandings, which made it almost impossible to reconcile their differences. May be, for new generation of Muslims, the best way to move forward is to accept the fundamental and permanent nature of the Quran, and judge everything else, including the *Hadith*, on that scale. May Allah SWT guide all of us to the right path.

With the above understanding, following is an effort to find the underlying principles of Islamic finance, including *Riba*. These are the main rules and are not all-inclusive. Also, for the sake of conciseness, and to avoid too much distraction, I have avoided providing every *hadith* or the reference in the Quran providing basis for these rules. Maybe, *InshaAllah*, it will coax some readers to review that material on their own.

#1: Dignified Living

The main purpose of business or any financial activity is to earn a living. While working or earning resources, there is no limit in Islam on what a person may earn or maintain but we are also reminded to avoid greed and be modest. Charitable activities are strongly recommended, especially towards those not able to work or earn a living (e.g., orphans or the physically or mentally disabled) or otherwise deprived of resources (e.g., destitute, travelers or prisoners). The preferred or recommended way of life is to work, earn one's own resources, and stay within one's means. These basic recommendations about the value of dignified living are critical both for an individual or a society, to avoid negative repercussions of laziness and irresponsibility on one hand, and over-spending and greed on the other.

Emphasizing the need, value, and significance of earned living; the Quran allows business activity even on the day of *Jumah* (Al-Quran 62:10), except during the *salat* time, and during the Hajj (Al-Quran 2:198). Further, guidance for these matters is provided by the Prophet SAW himself, through his own practical example, and as alluded in some of the following a*hadith*:

> Sahih Al Bukhari[2], Vol. 286: Narrated Al-Miqdam RA: The Prophet SAW said, "Nobody has ever

eaten a better meal than that which one has earned by working with one's own hands. The Prophet of Allah, David AS, used to eat from the earnings of his manual labor."

Sahih Al Bukhari[2], Vol. 3, 288: Narrated Abu Hurairah RA: Allah's Apostle SAW said, "One would rather cut and carry a bundle of wood on his back than ask somebody who may or may not give him."

Sahih Al Bukhari[2], Vol. 3, 285: Narrated Aishah RA: The companions of Allah's Messenger SAW used to practice manual labor, so their sweat used to smell, and they were advised to take a bath.

Sunan Ibn Majah, Vol. 3, Chapter 12, 2138: It was narrated from Miqdam bin Ma'dikarib (Az-Zubaidi) that the Messenger of Allah SAW said: "No man earns anything better than that which he earns with his own hands, and what a man spends on himself, his wife, his child and his servant, then it is charity."

Sunan Ibn Majah, Vol. 3, Chapter 12, 2142: It was narrated from Abu Humaid As-Sa'idi that the Messenger of Allah SAW said: "Be moderate in seeking worldly things, for everyone will be facilitated for which he was created."

Sunan Ibn Majah, Vol. 3, Chapter 12, 2410: Suhab Al-Khair narrated that the Messenger of Allah SAW said: "Any man who takes out a loan, having resolved not to pay it back, will meet Allah as a thief."

Sunan Ibn Majah, Vol. 3, Chapter 12, 2412: It was narrated from Thawban, the freed slave of the Messenger of Allah SAW, that the Messenger of Allah SAW said: "Anyone whose soul leaves his body, and he is free of three things, will enter Paradise: Arrogance, stealing from the spoils of war, and debt."

Sunan Abu Dawud, Chapter 22, 3343: It was narrated that Jabir said: "The Messenger of Allah SAW would not offer the funeral prayer for a man who had died in debt . . . ."

It is important to mention that the above recommendations are applicable to everyone, both men and women. There is no Islamic justification in the Quran or the *Hadith*, of any prohibition or any restriction upon women to engage in financial activities. In this regard, women are free to be independent and self-sufficient, and do not require a supervising 'man' or 'elder' or a *'wali'*. The appalling disparity between the fiscal outlook of men and women, especially in the 'Islamic' countries, has multiple reasons, including not complying with the Islamic rules of inheritance, systemic discrimination, and enforced customs and traditions, but all that without any religious basis, for the self-serving interests of men.

Value of material resources and personal responsibility is also emphasized in a different manner. This is about someone with meagre resources trying to do charity while he or she does not have enough means for sustenance. This type of charity is not recommended, for someone who may not afford it (Sahih Bukhari[2], Vol. 3, 598.) At the same time, it is recorded that the Prophet

SAW said that begging is forbidden by Allah SWT (Sahih Bukhari[2], Vol. 3, 591).

#2: Establishing Justice and Rejecting Injustice

Establishing justice in personal and communal life, and stopping injustice, is a fundamental Islamic principle, which applies to every aspect of our life. There are numerous *ayat* in the Quran promoting justice while discouraging, rejecting or outlawing injustice. There are many references describing the higher (worldly and spiritual) position of a just person or people, in this world and the Hereafter. The following two *ayat* about this subject are reflective of Allah SWT's position outlined in the Quran:

The Quran, Al-Nisa, *ayah* 135 (Al-Quran 4:135)

> "O ye who believe! Stand out firmly for justice, as witnesses to Allah, even as against yourselves, or your parents, or your kin, and whether it be (against) rich or poor: For Allah can best protect both. Follow not the lusts (Of your hearts), lest ye swerve, and if ye distort (justice) or decline to do justice, verily Allah is well-acquainted with all that ye do." Ali.

> "O you who believe! Stand out firmly for justice, as witnesses to Allah, even though it be against yourselves, or your parents, or your kin, be he rich or poor, Allah is a Better Protector to both (than you). So follow not the lusts (of your hearts), lest you may avoid justice, and if you distort your witness or refuse to give it, verily, Allah is Ever Well Acquainted with what you do." Al-Hilali & Khan.

The Islamic Finance and the Riba

The Quran, Al-Maidah, *ayah* 8 (Al-Quran 5:8)

> "O ye who believe! Stand out firmly for Allah, as witnesses to fair dealing, and let not the hatred of others to you make you swerve to wrong and depart from justice. Be just: that is next to Piety: and fear Allah. For Allah is well-acquainted with all that ye do." Ali.

> "O you who believe! Stand out firmly for Allah and be just witnesses and let not the enmity and hatred of others make you avoid justice. Be just: that is nearer to piety, and fear Allah. Verily, Allah is Well-Acquainted with what you do." Ali-Hilali & Khan.

Islamic concept of justice is accompanied by mercy, or *ihsaan*. Justice is the minimum requirement and *ihsaan* is always preferred, both in worldly and spiritual matters.

Business and finance, especially transactions with risk of *Riba*, involve close dealings between people and there always are chances of injustice, fraud, or deceit if proper rules are not in place. Whatever arrangement one may come up with, both for business and personal transactions, it must comply with the fundamental principle of justice. Justice is the rule for all parties involved, including the lender and the borrower, the merchant and the customer, without any overt or covert injustice, deceit, or fraud. For example, to avoid *Riba*, a financial arrangement must be just for all parties involved: the borrower(s) and the lender(s), or the parties making any financial transaction, or formulating a financial or business contract.

Allah SWT encouraged business and rejected acquiring other people's resources from illegal means:
Al-Quran, Al-Baqarah, *ayah* 275 (Al-Quran 2:275):

> "But Allah hath permitted trade and forbidden usury." Ali.

> "Whereas Allah has permitted trading and forbidden *Riba* (usury)." Al-Hilali & Khan.

Al-Quran, An-Nisa, ayah 29 (Al-Quran 4:29):

> "O ye who believe eat not up your property among yourselves in vanities; but let there be amongst you traffic and trade . . . " Ali.

> "O you who believe! Eat not up your property among yourselves unjustly except it be a trade amongst you." Al-Hilali & Khan.

Aside from many other forms of illegal financial gains, the practice of an unfair charge for a loan (usury) is considered unjust to the borrower, as the risk of a loss (for a business or commercial loan) is not equally shared between the lender and the borrower. This issue is discussed in detail above.

Finally, it is important to mention that there can be multiple ways or shades of injustice. The following *hadith* provides a different example:

> Sahih Bukhari[2] Vol. 3, 585: Narrated by Abu Huraira RA: Allah's Apostle SAW said, "Procrastination (delay) in repaying debts by a wealthy person is injustice."

#3: Proper Documentation

For a system to run smoothly, especially a financial system with money and assets at stake, and to avoid any problems and conflicts, it is utmost important to have proper documentation of all financial arrangements and transactions. The Quran is clear about this subject, and in fact the longest *ayah* of the Quran is about this issue:

The Quran, Al-Baqarah, *ayah* 282 (Al-Quran 2:282)

> "O ye who believe! When ye deal with each other, in transactions involving future obligations in a fixed period of time, reduce them to writing; let a scribe write down faithfully between the parties; let not the scribe refuse to write: as Allah has taught him, so let him write. Let him who incurs the liability dictate. But let him fear his Lord Allah, and not diminish aught of what he owes. If the party liable is mentally deficient, or weak, or unable himself to dictate, let his guardian dictate faithfully. And get two witnesses, out of your own men, and if there are not two men, then a man and two women, such as ye choose, for witnesses, so that if one of them errs, the other can remind her. The witnesses should not refuse when they are called on (for evidence). Disdain not to reduce to writing (your contract) for a future period. Whether it be small or big: it is juster in the sight of Allah, more suitable as evidence, and more convenient to prevent doubts among yourselves but if it be a transaction which ye carry out on the spot among yourselves there is no blame on you if ye reduce it not to writing. But take witnesses whenever ye make

a commercial contract; and let neither scribe nor witness suffer harm. If ye do (such harm), it would be wickedness in you. So fear Allah; for it is Allah that teaches you. And Allah is well acquainted with all things." Ali.

"O you who believe! When you contract a debt for a fixed period, write it down. Let a scribe write it down in justice between you. Let not the scribe refuse to write as Allah has taught him, so let him write. Let him (the debtor) who incurs the liability dictate, and he must fear Allah, his Lord, and diminish not anything of what he owes. But if the debtor is of poor understanding, or weak, or is unable himself to dictate, then let his guardian dictate in justice. And get two witnesses out of your own men. And if there are not two men (available), then a man and two women, such as you agree for witnesses, so that if one of them (two women) errs, the other can remind her. And the witnesses should not refuse when they are called on (for evidence). You should not become weary to write it (your contract), whether it be small or big, for its fixed term, that is more just with Allah; more solid as evidence, and more convenient to prevent doubts among yourselves, save when it is a present trade which you carry out on the spot among yourselves, then there is no sin on you if you do not write it down. But take witnesses whenever you make a commercial contract. Let neither scribe nor witness suffer any harm, but if you do (such harm), it would be wickedness in you. So be afraid of Allah; and Allah teaches you. And Allah is the All-Knower of each and everything." Al-Hilali and Khan.

Despite explicit instructions in the Quran, it is my observation that people routinely hesitate or disagree to write down arrangements of a business deal, or a private debt, especially within the family where the chances of conflict are same, if not higher. Many feel especially uncomfortable involving witnesses. On the other hand, people do it if it is required by a country's law. It shall be clear to every Muslim that, based upon this unequivocal *ayah* of the Quran, proper documentation is an explicit requirement for any such deal. The *ayah* also provides some directions to make this process as just and fair, and as transparent as possible. The purpose of all this is to avoid any financial, physical, and emotional harm to all parties involved. This practice also provide basis for a smoothly operating financial system.

#4: Avoidance of *Grahar*

The term *gharar* means avoidable uncertainty, which, if not avoided, may lead to *dharar* or injustice to a trading party. One may argue that every trade carries an element of uncertainty, or that at least some level of uncertainty is unavoidable. The concept of *gharar* addresses situations where uncertainty may not be that ambiguous and trading parties may even be aware of it. Buying an unborn animal, or fruit that is not yet ripe, are classic examples derived from the *Hadith*. While buying an unborn animal, it is impossible to fully predict its nature, or whether it is even going to be born alive, etc. Paying for the fruit of a tree before it is ripe also carry multiple uncertainties. Fruit can be affected by the weather or the blight. These types of situations create avoidable uncertainties, and the recommendation is to make the trade after the baby animal is born and inspected by the prospective buyer, or when the fruit is ripe and inspected.

Finally, one shall also note that the concept of *gharar* is not about any deceit and fraud, overt or covert, which also is categorically illegal.

> Sahih Muslim Vol. 4, [3851] 42 – (1530). Jabir bin Abdullah said: "The Messenger of Allah SAW forbade selling of heap of dates, the weight of which is unknown, for a known weight of dates."
>
> Sahih Muslim Vol. 4, [3865] 51 – (1534). It was narrated that Ibn Umar said: "The Messenger of Allah SAW said: 'Do not sell produce until its goodness appears and there is no longer fear of blight.'"
>
> Sunan Abu Dawud, Vol. 4, 3372. Yunus said: "I asked Abu Az-Zinad about selling crops before they are ripe and what was said about that. He said: "Urwah bin Az-Zubair narrated from Sahl bin Abi Hatmah, that Zaid bin Thabit said: "The people used to sell crops before they were ripe, then when the people harvested the crop and payment was demanded, the buyer would say:
>
> "It has been stricken with *Duman*, or *Qusham* or *Murad* – types of blight concerning which they disputed. When many disputes were referred to the Prophet SAW, the Messenger of Allah SAW said, as if offering advice: 'No, do not sell crops until they have ripened" because there were too many disputes and differences among them." (Sahih)
>
> Sunan Abu Dawud, Vol. 4, 3375. It was narrated from Jabir bin Abdullah that the Prophet SAW forbade *Al-Muawamah*. And one of them (the narrators) said: "selling years in advance." (Sahih)

> Sunan Abu Dawud, Vol. 4, 3376. It was narrated From Abu Hurairah that the Prophet SAW forbade transactions involving ambiguity *(Gharar)*. (Sahih)
>
> Sunan Ibn Majah, Vol. 3, 2195: It was narrated that Ibn 'Abbas said: "The Messenger of Allah SAW forbade *gharar* transactions."
>
> Sunan Ibn Majah, Vol. 3, 2170: It was narrated from Abu Sa'eed Al-Khudri that the Messenger of Allah SAW forbade Mulamasah and Munabadhah. Sahl said: "Sufyan said: 'Mulamasah means when a man touches something with his hand without seeing it, and Munabadhah means when he says: "Toss me what you have, and I will toss you what I have."

In a different example, bartering of one type of dates with another kind was prohibited. It was advised to sell one type and use the proceeds to buy the second kind. Bringing the requirement of selling one item and using the proceeds to buy the second (similar one) helped to minimize market price related doubts and disputes. This kind of transaction may also proceed on the spot if both parties check or are aware of the market price of their products, and transaction is made based upon the prices of their products instead of volume or weight. Bartering of fungible items is permitted if the items are not of the same type. This rule is better understood and applicable to fungible items and not as much to non-fungible ones. One shall also note another important aspect of this type of transaction, the fact that it is without the concept of deferment, as the deal is made on the spot or hand-to-hand. In addition, there is no extra amount, or 'interest' involved, but even then, it is not permitted, and is considered a *Riba* transaction.

#5: Encouraging Trade

The Quran, Al-Nisa, *ayah* 29 (Al-Quran 4:29)
> "O ye who believe! Eat not up your property among yourself in vanities; but let there be amongst you traffic and trade by mutual good will . . . " Ali

> "O you who believe! Eat not up your property among yourselves unjustly except it be a trade amongst you, by mutual consent . . . " Al-Hilali & Khan.

Islam specifically promote trade or business on both at personal and societal level, which helps to move the capital around in the society, with its multiple benefits. Islamic way of life and rules promote investing the capital, instead of its waste or hoarding, which benefits both the investor and the society. Trading or business was the major profession for pre-Islamic Arabs and the early Muslim society of Madinah. Numerous *ahadith* were documented about different aspects of trading and business, covering multiple topics. In addition, commercial activities are allowed even on the day of *Jumah*, and during Hajj.

While trade is encouraged, some related activities are either deemed illegal, such as, the *Riba,* unlawful acquisition or seizure of property, hoarding of commodities or resources, etc.; or disapproved, such as wasting resources. It is state's responsibility to create safe and secure business environment, establish proper business regulations and their implementation, and, at minimum, not be a hindrance to free trade. State controlled business institutions, improper taxation, and lack of proper legal framework are the main factors impacting business in many struggling-to-develop societies.

6: Avoidance of *Dharar*

While encouraging commercial activities, we are asked to observe strict fairness standards to avoid any *dharar*, the avoidable financial harm or loss:

The Quran, Al-Isra, *ayah* 35 (Al-Quran 17:35)

> "Give full measure when ye measure, and weigh with a balance that is straight: that is the most fitting and the most advantageous in the final determination." Ali

> "And give full measure when you measure, and weigh with a balance that is straight. That is good (advantageous) and better in the end." Al-Hilali & Khan.

The Quran, Ar-Rahman, *ayah* 8-9 (Al-Quran 55:8-9)

> "In order that ye may not transgress (due) balance. So establish weight with justice and fall not short in the balance." Ali.

> "In order that you may not transgress (due) balance. And observe the weight with equity and do not make the balance deficient." Al-Hilali & Khan.

#7: Prohibition of Fraud and Deceit

Any type of fraud and deceit, more specifically in business, are outlawed by the Quran:

The Quran, Al-Mutaffifin, *ayah* 1-3 (Al-Quran 83:1-3)

> "Woe to those that deal in fraud- those who, when they have to receive by measure from men, exact full measure. But when they have to give by measure or weight to men, give less than due." Ali.

> "Woe to *Al-Mutaffifun* (those who give less in measure and weight). Those who, when they have to receive by measure from men, demand full measure, and when they have to give by measure or weight to (other) men, give less than due." Al-Hilali & Khan.

A Muslim must not hide any defect of the product being traded, as trading in deceit, in addition to the *dharar* (loss) to the other party, may accomplish a sale but can lead to long-term damage to the trust and goodwill between the trading parties. In addition, it carries the burden of not following Allah SWT's instructions, resulting in loss of His blessings, and incurring His anger.

There are numerous examples in the *Hadith* where the Prophet SAW specifically disapproved many types of overt or covert deceitful sales or trading practices. It is the selfishness and greed that may tempt people to deal in this error, instead of the trust in Allah SWT and his recommended ways. Anyone resisting and rejecting this sin may bring peace, prosperity, and multiple other benefits to himself and the society. Historically, it is the Muslim traders, instead of religious clergy, whose conduct impressed people of far-away places benefiting them and bringing people to the religion. Even now, the situation is not any different, people are more interested or influenced by the conduct of trading or service, instead of arguments or speeches.

#8: Prohibition of *Riba*

Islam categorically prohibits *Riba*. The instructions for its prohibition directly and explicitly are derived from the Quran (Al-Quran 2:278-279). It is considered one of the major sins, and the Quran provides statement of a declaration of war in this life, between the person indulging in *Riba* and Allah SWT, and vivid description of the terrible fate in afterlife, waiting for someone consuming it. There is room for atonement if the person returns anything obtained illegally and avoids any further indulgence. The subject of the basis and nature of *Riba* is expansive and is discussed in detail in this writing.

#9: Respect of Capital Ownership

Ownership of personal property and wealth is a protected right in Islam. One is allowed to fight defending his or her estate and considered a martyr if killed in that process.

The Prophet SAW's last sermon:

> "Verily your blood, your property are as sacred and inviolable as the sacredness of this day of yours, in this month of yours, in this town of yours."

The Quran, Al-Hajj, *ayah* 39 (Al-Quran 22:39):
"To those against whom war is made, permission is given (to fight), because they are wronged – and verily, Allah is Most Powerful for their aid." Ali.

"Permission to fight is given to those (i.e. believers against disbelievers), who are fighting them, (and) because they (believers) have been wronged, and surely, Allah is Able to give them (believers) victory." Al-Hilali & Khan.

There is also the concept of societal ownership of common spaces and assets (like public land, roads, parks or rivers), but the state or the government is not allowed to usurp anyone's wealth or ownership without a valid reason or without just compensation. Islam does not put a limit on earning or owning any amount of wealth or estate if no prohibited means are used to acquire them, Zakat is paid, and any other laws are followed. In this manner, Islam starkly differs from communism and is like the so-called 'capitalism' with, aside from many others, an obvious exception of the *Riba*.

#10: Redistribution of Wealth

Islam is concerned about the accumulation of wealth by a select few:

The Quran, Al-Hashr, *ayah* 7 (Al-Quran 59:7)

" . . . in order that it may not (merely) make a circuit between the wealthy among you . . . " Ali.

" . . . in order that it may not become a fortune used by the rich among you . . . " Al-Hilali & Khan.

While allowing earning, owning, or maintaining any amount of assets or estate, the concern about the accumulation or concentration of wealth in a select few hands is also addressed, mainly by establishing the *Zakat* system. The Zakat, a 2.5% assessment, is a religious obligation on accumulated wealth or estate, paid once a year. It enables transfer of wealth from the rich to the neediest. In addition, Islamic inheritance rules are different, with promotion and allocation of estate to multiple potential heirs instead of a generational single-family control. These practices establish a system for at least partial dissemination of capital within the community. In addition, there is almost continuous emphasis in the Quran on spending money in charitable causes.

Like the above concept is disapproval of idling a potential resource of food or wealth. For example, it is disapproved to leave a piece of cultivable land without use, while some needy people in the vicinity may utilize it for their sustenance. While earning a fortune or building any amount of enterprise or an estate is not necessarily un-Islamic, erecting an idled pile of cash or gold is against its spirit.

#11: Rights of Bankruptcy

Aside from making money or earning profit, financial loss is a common business reality. Businesses and ventures may fail due to multiple reasons, despite the best of intentions and honest practices. Failed ventures can result in irredeemable debts and a person may not be able to pay back a loan. Islam has provided ways to manage such situations.

> Sahih Muslim Vol 4, Chapter 4, [3991] 18 – (1556). It was narrated that Abu Saeed Al Khudri

said: "At the time of the Messenger of Allah SAW, a man suffered loss of some fruit that he had bought, and his debts mounted. The Messenger of Allah said: 'Give him charity,' and the people gave him charity, but it was not enough to pay off his debt. The Messenger of Allah said to his creditors: 'Take what you find, and you are not entitled to any more than that.'"

This *hadith* provides the basis for bankruptcy laws, which are part of every modern financial system. These laws are designed to maintain a system where people are encouraged to invest in business, not afraid to take risks but also not afraid of (within reason) losing personal health and home, in case a venture fails. The Islamic perspective on this subject is more towards generosity than restrictiveness:

> Sunan Ibn Majah, Vol. 3, Chapter 33, 2219: It was narrated from Jabir bin 'Abdullah that the Messenger of Allah SAW said: "Whoever sells fruits then the crop fails, should not take any of his brother's money. Why would any of you take the money of his Muslim brother?"

In the USA, personal and business bankruptcy is not an uncommon occurrence. In general, the laws around it are on the generous side, and protect every party's personal health and essential private possessions, such as the primary home and an automobile.

#12: No Trade Without Full Possession

According to this rule, one may not sell something that one does not own, or does not have the possession of, especially the food or the fungible items. Sometimes people purchase something, especially a fungible item and, without taking its possession, re-sell it. This practice is not allowed in Islam. Similarly, one may not try to sell a home or a car for which one has not taken the possession of. The rule shall be understood correctly, as it does not mean that one may not plan to buy a home not yet built, or a car not yet manufactured, or a crop not yet grown. In the former case, while trying to sell a car without its possession, someone is either trying to cheat (*dharar*), or is taking a significant but avoidable risk (*gharar*), making both transactions problematic. In the latter case, when someone is ordering a home to be built or a crop to be delivered, there is an underlying necessity or a reason (the builder or the farmer, both need resources to start their work) beneficial to both parties, and the larger society. Though there may still be risk involved, the benefit is higher, and the risk can be minimized with a proper legal contract.

In this manner, when the intention of the contract is more than just making money, without any harm to either party, and if applied intelligently, it helps to foster businesses such as agriculture and manufacturing. On the other hand, if the intention is to make money with no other specific consideration or benefit to society, with avoidable risk to one party, such as the conventional trading in derivatives, it frequently leads to personal and societal ruins.

> Sunan Ibn Majah, Vol. 3, Chapter 20, 2187: It was narrated that Hakim bin Hizam said: "I said: 'O Messenger of Allah, a man is asking me to sell him something that I do not possess. Shall I sell it to him? He said: 'Do not sell what is not with you.' "

> Sunan Ibn Majah, Vol. 3, Chapter 20, 2188: It was narrated from 'Amr bin Shu'aib, from his father, that his grandfather said: "The Messenger of Allah SAW said: 'It is not permissible to sell something that is not with you, nor to profit from what you do not possess.'"

> Sunan Ibn Majah, Vol. 3, Chapter 49, 2257: " . . . Usamah bin Zaid told me that the Messenger of Allah SAW said: "Usury is only in credit."

It is also clear that in some situations this principle is applied differently. For example, it is allowed to make arrangement for purchase of something in advance (something that does not exist at the time of the business contract) if its benefit is larger than the risk it may carry, as in the following hadith:

> Sunan Abu Dawud, Chapter 22, 3463: It was narrated that Ibn Abbas said: "When the Messenger of Allah SAW came to Al-Madinah, they used to pay one or two or three years in advance for dates. The Messenger of Allah SAW said: 'Whoever pays in advance for dates, let him pay for a specified measure and a specified weight, (to be delivered) at a specified time.'"

One application of this principle, on a larger scale, is the restriction on a bank to not lend an amount it does not have, or it can safely lend. As money is a fungible item and the banks are not required to hold every individual deposit, they are at least required to have assets to match the amount of those deposits, or to match the loans they are offering. This is a generally agreed upon fiscal principle unless it is ignored, which at one time

The Islamic Finance and the Riba

was thought to be one of the main causes of widespread financial collapse and recession in the U.S.A.

#13: Contractual Obligations

Being trustworthy and fulfilling contractual responsibilities is a fundamental Islamic requirement and trait. The Prophet SAW was known for his truthfulness and trustworthiness even before he announced his Prophethood. The Quran is explicitly clear about this subject, as follows:

The Quran, Al-Maidah, *ayah* 1 (Al-Quran 5:1)
"O ye who believe! Fulfill (all) obligations." Ali.
"O you who believe! Fulfill (your) obligations." Al-Hilali & Khan.

While the Quranic message is precise and comprehensive, the *Hadith* provides some detail of its application in business and finance:

> Sunan Ibn-Majah, Chapter 12, 2181: It was narrated from 'Abdullah bin 'Umar that the Messenger of Allah SAW said: "When two men enter into a transaction, each of them has the choice (of annulling it) so long as they have not yet parted and are still together, or one of them has given the option or choice to the other. Once he has accepted the terms of the other, then the transaction is binding. If they part after concluding the transaction and neither of them has rescinded the transaction, then the transaction is binding."

> Sahih Al-Bukhara, Chapter 34, 2113: Narrated Ibn Umar RA, "The Prophet SAW said, 'No deal

is settled and finalized unless the buyer and the seller separate, except if the deal is optional (whereby the validity of the bargain depends upon the stipulations agreed upon).'"

#14: No Imposition Without Justification

As per this rule, which applies to every part of Islamic life, nothing is mandated or not allowed (declared *haram*) unless it is clearly stated, explicitly or implicitly, in the Quran or the *Hadith*. For matters of fundamental beliefs and worship or *ibadah*, compulsory innovations are not allowed as they are specifically prohibited. For other more practical or worldly matters, the default option is to provide ease, and a restriction is applied only if stated. Anything that is not clearly prohibited, is not part of fundamental acts of worship, and does not have any conflict with fundamentals of beliefs, may not be completely restricted. An unwarranted prohibition is also considered an innovation in religion, which is not permissible:

The Quran, Al-Maidah, *ayah* 3 (Al-Quran 5:3):
"... This day have I perfected your religion for you ... " Ali.

"... This day, I have perfected your religion for you ... " Al-Hilali & Khan.

The Quran, Al-Nisa, *ayah* 171 (Al-Quran 4:171):
"O People of the Book! Commit no excesses in your religion ... " Ali.

"O people of the Scripture (Jews and Christians)! Do not exceed the limits in your religion ... " Al-Hilali & Khan.

The Quran, Al-Maidah, *ayah* 77 (Al-Quran 5:77):
> "Say: "O people of the Book! Exceed not in your religion the bounds (of what is proper), trespassing beyond the truth, nor follow the vain desires of people who went wrong in times gone by – who mislead many, and strayed (themselves) from the even Way." Ali.

> "Say (O Muhammad SAW): "O people of the Scripture (Jews and Christians)! Exceed not the limits in your religion (by believing in something) other than the truth, and do not follow the vain desires of people who went astray in times gone by, and who misled many, and strayed (themselves) from the Right Path." Al-Hilali & Khan.

> Sunan Abu Dawud, Vol. 5, 4607: The Messenger of Allah SWT said, " . . . And beware of newly-invented matters, for every newly-invented matter is an innovation and every innovation is a deviation."

This rule is applicable in rare situations, and due to its nature, is prone to a variety of opinions and controversy. For example: Is it allowed to have a bank account? The banks, in an institutionalized form we know today, did not exist centuries ago. To safeguard their assets or money, people trusted their family, friends, or some people more than others. It is not clear though if there was a charge for this service, or if it was done in an institutionalized manner with central rules and regulations. As there was no stated or exemplified, explicit or implicit, prohibition in the Quran and the *Hadith* about it, establishing a bank cannot be forbidden. People agreeing with this opinion may emphasize the benefits of a banking institution, while the ones against, may talk more about its *Riba*-laden business practices.

#15: The Partnerships

Doing business in partnership is allowed and in fact recommended, instead of wasting resources or trying to harm each other. The Quran provides specific instructions about this issue:

The Quran, Al Nisa, *ayah* 29 (Al-Quran 4:29)

> "O ye who believe! Eat not up your property among yourselves in vanities; but let there be amongst you traffic and trade by mutual good will: Nor kill (or destroy) yourselves: for verily Allah hath been to you Most Merciful!" Ali.
> "O you who believe! Eat not up your property among yourselves unjustly except it be a trade amongst you, by mutual consent. And do not kill yourselves (nor kill one another). Surely, Allah is Most Merciful to you." Al-Hilali & Khan

It is important to mention that even in a partnership, basic Islamic rules of fairness are still applicable. Partners may share in profit and loss, equally or at whatever terms they agree upon, but it may not include a fixed benefit to one or more investors irrespective of profit or loss in the business, or any other unjust arrangement. This is tantamount to *dharar* to the other partner(s), which is not allowed.

An investor may also hire someone to invest on his or her behalf, like an agent, but that is more of an employment than a partnership. In case of a total or significant loss, the investor may lose its investment, and the agent his knowhow, time and labor. This is the same arrangement people now use for venture capital projects. The Prophet SAW probably profited from a similar arrangement when he worked for Khadija bint Khuwaylid RA (her resources and his labor and knowhow), before she accepted Islam and married him.

One related issue to the partnership is the matter of *Shufa* or pre-emption in joint properties or joint ventures. The right of pre-emption is seldom valid in these days, as matters and boundaries are clearly defined, or they should have been clearly defined. It may be a defensible right of a partner, if underlying details are not clearly defined.

> Sahih Bukhari[2], Vol. 3, 458: Narrated Jaber bin Abdullah RA: Allah's Apostle SAW gave a verdict regarding *Shufa* in every undivided joint thing (property). But if the limits are defined (or demarcated) or the ways and streets are fixed, then there is no pre-emption.

This *hadith* also implies that in usual business ventures, where resources and matters are not clearly defined, one partner carries the right of pre-emption over the other, in case of a split.

#16: Prohibition of Gambling

Gambling is mentioned here because it can be a significant part of a business, or it by itself can be the business. It is specifically prohibited in Islam. There are multiple ways or form of gambling, and the Quran and the *Hadith* described some of them. By analogy, all similar practices are prohibited.

The Quran, Al Baqarah, *ayah* 218 (Al-Quran 2:218):

> "They ask thee concerning wine and gambling. Say: "In them is great sin, and some benefit, for men; but the sin is greater than the benefit." Ali. "They ask you (O Muhammad SAW) concerning alcoholic drink and gambling. Say: "In them is a great sin, and (some) benefit for men, but the sin of them is greater than their benefit." Al-Hilali & Khan.

The Quran, Al Maidah, *ayah* 90-91 (Al-Quran 5:90-91):
> "O ye who believe! Intoxicants and gambling, (dedication of) arrows, are an abomination – of Satan's handiwork; eschew such (abomination), that ye may prosper. Satan's plan is (but) to excite enmity and hatred between you, with intoxicants and gambling, and hinder you from the remembrance of Allah, and from prayer: will ye not then abstain?"

> "O you who believe! Intoxicants (all kinds of alcoholic drinks), gambling, *Al-Ansab*, and *Al-Azlam* (arrows for seeking luck or decision) are an abomination of *Shaitan*'s (Satan) handiwork. So avoid (strictly all) that (abomination) in order that you may be successful. *Shaitan* (Satan) wants only to excite enmity and hatred between you with intoxicants (alcoholic drinks) and gambling, and hinder you from the remembrance of Allah and from *As-Salat* (the prayer). So, will you not then abstain?" Al-Hilali & Khan.

There were multiple ways people used the idea of gambling in old days. One example was about deciding with arrows. For example, after an animal was killed, the hunting party, instead of dividing it either equally or based upon the effort put, decided everyone's share by a lottery using arrows. Doing it this way, even if there was no fraud or deceit, some got nothing, or less than what they deserved, and other more than what was right. One may easily understand the injustice and the resulting ill-will between the group afterwards. This type of practice is not permitted, and the recommendation is to use an alternate and just way of making such decisions.

#17: The Taxation

The concept of taxation, as currently understood and practiced all over the world, including most Muslim countries, is not necessarily entirely Islamic. This subject is large and complicated, not directly relevant to this writing, and not discussed in detail here. Despite that, the issue of taxation is inter-twined with finance and cannot be ignored.

The tax, as defined in the dictionary, meant, "a compulsory contribution to state revenue, levied by the government on workers' income and business profits, or added to the cost of some goods, services, and transactions." There is a school of thought suggesting that there is no concept of "taxes" in Islam. According to them, there are a few defined ways an Islamic government acquired resources: a. A part, 1/5th, of the wealth obtained of the enemy in war, b. 5-10% income tax on agriculture, c. Taxing non-Muslims living in an Islamic system who may not serve in the military, d. Income generated by the public-owned assets, such as the land or other natural resources, and e. The *Zakat*, which is a 2.5% charge on assets, not on income. Muslims do not consider the *Zakat* as a tax; it is rather a religious obligation for those whose assets exceed a defined value. Also, in most cases, the *Zakat* can only be spent on certain well-defined areas, not on everything a state does. In an Islamic system, the taxes are paid by the ones who can afford, and not levied on everyone. Some people claim that if only a Muslim state establishes the above system, there may not be a need for any other tax, and the state can have enough resources to take care of people's affairs. Reviewing the finances of the state of Qatar, we may agree with this notion, in many other places, it seems a doubtful notion.

Besides many other, there are a few key responsibilities of any modern state government, e.g., the defense, law & order, taking care of its sick and poor, and clean environment including water & plumbing. Out of the list of sources of income provided above, the only realistic avenues for a state to generate income are the 5-10% tax on agriculture, or the income from the public assets. On the other hand, citizens' expectations from the state are also unrealistic. Muslim societies in general are mired by the conflict of rights versus responsibilities, both within the governments and its citizens. The rights: everyone is sure about; it is the responsibilities people struggled with.

If the concept of income-tax means taxing everyone earning money, or taxing every dollar generated, it is against the principles and spirit of Islam. The reason for not taxing everyone or the ones barely making their ends meet is not because they cannot or shall not do charity. Charity is an entirely different and voluntary concept, which Islam strongly recommends in variety of ways, though not for the ones who may not afford it. Of note, the tax on the agriculture income is not considered a charity either. There is no specific or explicit restriction in Islam against taxing high earners, people or businesses, provided this practice follows the rules of fairness and justice.

At the end, whatever the concept of taxation might be, it must follow the fundamental rules of Islam, many of them described above. There is no specific reference about taxation in the Quran (charity is a different matter). Based upon at least two *ahadith* I came across, a specific type of taxation is forbidden. The first is a part of a long *hadith* in Sahih Muslim where the Prophet SAW commented about the status of a woman being punished for *zina* (illegal sexual encounter), and he indirectly described the gravity of wrong associated with what was described as *Maks:*

> Sahih Muslim, Vol. 4, 4432: " . . . . Calm down, O Khalid! By the One in Whose Hand is my soul, she has repented in such a manner that if the *Maks* – collector repented like that, he would be forgiven."

Following is the second *hadith:*
> Musnad of Imam Ahmad bin Hanbal, Vol. 28, 17001: "Indeed, associates of *Maks* (the one charging it) were of the Fire."

The real issue is the meaning of the word and the concept of *"Maks"*, as was understood at that time. In the footnote of the translation of Sahih Bukhari, it is described as, "an unjust tax collected by the helpers of the wrongdoers when people buy and sell." In both *ahadith*, the way it is mentioned, it represented an activity by individual(s), not the state or the government, though one may argue that it can be applied to the state too. In many repressive societies, led by the corrupt or wrongly guided politicians, or the local mafia, it is not uncommon to find such illegal practices or "taxation". People are forced to pay a charge while trading or moving their crops or products from one place to the other, sometimes while bringing them to the marketplace for direct sale to the consumer. Islam recommends uninterrupted flow of goods, as much as possible, directly by the farmer or the producer to the marketplace to avoid any illegal taxation or a charge or profiteering by an intermediary. Instead of charging an illegal levy or a tax, it is the state's responsibility to facilitate an environment guaranteeing free flow of goods without any injustice to individuals or businesses, which ultimately benefit all consumers and the society, and thus the state. Based upon the above *ahadith*, only a certain type of taxation or levy is outlawed, not of every kind.

It is a well-known fact that the governments may easily slide into corrupt practices and impose unnecessary or unjust taxes. In an Islamic state, every tax ordinance, aside from its political approval, is not valid if it violates any fundamentals of Islamic finance. The government may force it, declaring it the law, as is the situation in many Muslim countries. In the book of Allah SWT though, if it conflicts with His Law, it remains illegal with all its negative repercussions. One such example is taxation on sale of alcohol. One obvious lesson to learn from the above *ahadith* is that Islam, evidenced by the words of the Prophet SAW, has an extremely strong and forceful position against illegal taxation.

#18: The Worker's Rights

Part of any successful financial system or an enterprise is the way it deals with its work force. A system is only good enough or productive enough as its workers are.

Islamic rules do not allow any amount of injustice or harm to the workers. As merely the words were not enough, the Prophet SAW provided a practical example. First, no work was considered less dignified than others. The Prophet did everything in his house that a "servant" might do, tending his own animals, and mending his own shoes. Everyone lived and ate in the same dwellings, with no discrimination. Outside the house, he labored like anyone else. If resources were scarce, he suffered like everyone else, if not more. With his excellence of character and generosity, people working for him never wanted to leave even if that was a clearly stated option. Learning from his example, his associates followed the suit. According to the famous story, when the caliph Omar ibn Khattab, may Allah SWT be please with him, entered the city of Jerusalem with his servant, as the leader of the Islamic state, the locals could not differentiate between the servant and the master.

In more practical terms, one is required to discuss and finalize the exact labor or the wage before any work is done and mandated to pay it as soon as the work is accomplished. In terms of some modern concepts of worker's rights such as safe and healthy work environment, equality of pay between men and women, or health insurance, they are all applicable and covered under the requirement of justice and no harm. A Muslim employer is expected to provide similar, if not the same, benefits to his or her employees as to themselves. There is a famous *hadith* of the Prophet SAW:

> Sahih Al-Bukhari, Vol. 1, Chapter 2, 12: Narrated Anas RA: The Prophet SAW said, "None of you will have faith till he likes for his (Muslim) brother what he likes for himself".

Chapter 14 – The Rules of Islamic Finance

It is important to note that for fairness and justice to prevail, Islam does not make distinction between a Muslim or a non-Muslim. The Prophet SAW provided clear and unequivocal examples to make that point. It was tragic that many of these rights are routinely violated both in poor and affluent Muslim societies, and the workers many times are dealt more like slaves than a justly negotiated workforce.

#19: No Trading or Dealing in *Haram*

According to this rule, a Muslim may not deal, trade, or make a profit with something not allowed in Islam. Examples of such items are pork meat, alcoholic beverages, drugs of abuse (like opium, heroin, cocaine etc.), gambling, prostitution, the business of *Riba*, an unjust war, or any such illegal activity. Following references provide its basis:

The Quran, Al-Nisa, *ayah* 29 (Al-Quran 4:29:

> "O ye who believe! Eat not up your property among yourself in vanities; but let there be amongst you traffic and trade by mutual good will: Nor kill (or destroy) yourselves: for verily Allah hath been to you Most Merciful!" Ali.

> "O you who believe! Eat not up your property among yourselves unjustly except it be a trade amongst you, by mutual consent. And do not kill yourselves (nor kill one another). Surely, Allah is Most Merciful to you." Al-Hilali & Khan.

Both translations are somewhat restrictive and not conveying the comprehensive message, which some other scholars have suggested. The key words in the first part of the *ayah* are *amwaal* (translated as property) and *baatil* (translated as vanities or unjustly). *Amwaal* is the plural of *maal* with meanings of money, wealth, possessions, property, assets, fortunes, etc., and the word *baatil* means null, invalid, futile, vain, worthless, vanity, injustice, etc. The main message to the believers in the first part of the *ayah* is to not consume *amwaal* in *baatil* activities, which includes dealing in *haram*.

> Sahih Bukhari (translated by Hilal Yayinlari), Vol. 3, 429: Narrated Aisha RA: When the last verse of Surat-al-Baqara were revealed, the Prophet SAW went out (of the house to the Mosque) and said, "The trade of alcohol has become illegal."

> Sahih Muslim Vol. 4, Chapter 19, [4093] 106 – (1598). It was narrated that Jabir said: "The Messenger of Allah SAW cursed the one who consumes *Riba* and the one who pays (or deputize) it, the one who writes it down and the two who witness it," and he said: "They are all the same."

In a different *hadith*, the Prophet SAW declared earning of a prostitute illegal. Following this rule, one may not get into any part of such illegal businesses in any manner.

Sometimes understanding or application of this rule has resulted in a controversial situation. This is when a decision made by a Muslim, based upon this rule, indirectly affects someone else, especially a non-Muslim. Example of that may be a Muslim taxi-driver refusing to accept a passenger carrying a bottle of alcoholic beverage. Applying this rule in this manner is problematic, especially in a non-Muslim society, or in any society for that matter. The person hiring a cab is hiring it for his or her ride, not to transport the bottle in their possession. If on the other hand, the taxi-driver is asked to transport only the alcohol, refusal may be justified. In that case, it is like if a driver is asked to transport heroin or cocaine. In some other situations it may get tricky. For example, what if a prostitute hires a cab? Better option for the driver is to stay away from areas with suspicious activities. But if a situation arises where a ride like that is requested, his or her job is to provide the service and safely transport the passenger. If someone is still uncomfortable, he or she may refuse to accept the fare, or give it away in charity.

For a Muslim, especially someone living in a non-Muslim society, the way to solve this type of issue is to perform a realistic cost-benefit analysis, described underneath. This type of rule in Islam carries enough flexibility based upon the situation and the intention, as suggested by the following two *ahadith*:

> Sahih Bukhari[2], Vol. 1, 1: On the pulpit 'Umar bin Al-Khattab RA said: I heard Allah's Apostle SAW saying, "The reward of deeds depends upon the intentions and every person will get the reward according to what he has intended. So whoever emigrated for worldly benefits or for a woman to marry, his emigration was for what he emigrated for."

According to a different *hadith*, once the Prophet SAW was traveling with some people and they found a dead sheep. Apparently, as the meat of dead animal is *haram* to eat, no one touched the sheep. Noticing that, the Prophet SAW asked why they weren't interested in its skin, which was still usable for other purposes?

Sahih Bukhari[2], Vol. 3, 424: Narrated Abdullah bin Abbas RA: Once Allah's Apostle SAW passed by a dead sheep and said to the people, "Wouldn't you benefit by its skin?" The people replied that it was dead. The Prophet SAW said, "But only its eating is illegal."

Another example for understanding is of an intoxicant, such as opium, which is *haram* to deal with, but is also used for pain. In this manner, it is allowed to be in the business of making harmful chemicals but only if it is controlled and used for *halal* reasons.

#20: Cost-Benefit Analysis

In matters of human interactions, especially commerce, every day can bring a new set of challenges, at times due to natural reasons, and at times facilitated or created by human beings. It is a common tendency, both among critics and proponents of Islam, to consider Islamic laws as well-defined black and white concepts. The reality in fact is very different, instead of black and white, there always is a shade of gray.

Meat of swine is *haram*, but not when it can save a life. Washing face, hands and feet with water is mandatory before *salat*, but a similar dry act is allowed if water is not available. Praying on time with full set of *rakat* of five daily prayers is obligatory, but it may all be easily changed if circumstances are not conducive. Stealing is a punishable act, but the state may not punish a person stealing food out of poverty and hunger. Acts like fasting and Hajj are mandatory but may not be for someone with poor health or meager resources. The list can go on-and-on both for acts of *ibadah* or day-to-day living situations where Islam almost always provides flexibility for difficult, unpredictable, or uncontrollable situations. Reflecting deeper, one may find that whenever conventional rule is relaxed, and it is relaxed when it may not be possible to follow, the benefit of relaxation is heavier or larger than its cost. In analogical terms, whenever presented with a new, unclear, or difficult situation, a cost-benefit analysis is the way to reach the right conclusion. Here, one must emphasize that the *benefit* carries more weight in spiritual than in material terms, as the basic purpose of the faith is purification of the soul not just material benefit.

Al-Quran, Al-Ala, *ayah* 14 (Al-Quran 87:14)

> "But those will proser who purify themselves," Ali.

> "Indeed, whosoever purifies himself (by avoiding polytheism and accepting Islamic Monotheism) shall achieve success." Al-Hilali & Khan.

In general, one may not sell or trade something one does not have or possess, but this is allowed when making arrangement with a farmer or a manufacturer to buy products not yet grown or manufactured. The benefit of this arrangement outweighs its risks or the cost. In a different example, it is not recommended to trade un-ripe fruit on trees, until it is ripe or harvested to avoid any conflict, but it can be done if it has other benefits.

The concept of cost-benefit analysis is rooted in the Quranic principles and the *Hadith* (as alluded above):

The Quran, Al-Baqarah, *ayah* 185 (Al-Quran 2:185)

" . . . . Allah intends every facility for you; He does not want to put you to difficulties . . . ." Ali.

" . . . . Allah intends for you ease, and He does not want to make things difficult for you . . . ." Al-Hilali & Khan.

The Quran, Al-Maidah, *ayah* 6 (Al-Quran 5:6)
" . . . . Allah doth not wish to place you in a difficulty, ..." Ali.

" . . . . Allah does not want to place you in a difficulty, ..." Al-Hilali & Khan.

The Quran, Al-Baqarah, *ayah* 286 (Al-Quran 2:286)
"On no soul doth Allah place a burden greater than it can bear . . . ." Ali.

"Allah burdens not a person beyond his scope . . . ." Al-Hilali & Khan.

While an extremely important Islamic rule, because of its nature and implications, whenever invoked it may generate much debate and controversy. Following this rule, it is allowed to let a business make intoxicants or otherwise harmful chemicals used for medical purpose, graft trees to produce better and newer varieties (though that is changing their nature), allowing in-vitro fertilization for some couples with infertility, and, as per some scholars, allowance of *Riba* in non-Muslim societies.

#21: Borrowing or Taking a Debt

Borrowing is a common social and business activity. We may think that only poor people borrowed, but one can be surprised by its realistic analysis. Currently, the USA is one of the richest countries in the world with its economy bigger than any other, but its debt is also larger than any other country. Poor people borrow smaller and the rich a larger amount. Incurring the type of debt affecting rich people or the richer nations can be against Islamic principles. For example, a debt taken to gamble, or to own a car or a home one may not be able to afford is against Islamic principles. Modesty, patience, and living within the means are strong Islamic traits. At the same time, one is allowed to take a debt for genuine needs. Even the Prophet SAW and his associates, the one who were not rich, borrowed or took a debt. It is also allowed to borrow from a non-Muslim, the Prophet SAW did.

Excessive borrowing is discouraged but borrowing in general is allowed in Islam. One is not supposed to borrow an amount that he or she, or his or her estate after death, may not pay it off. The Prophet SAW refused to lead funeral prayer of someone whose debt was not paid off, in a way conveying his strong dislike for this behavior. Sometimes, though, emergencies can happen, and the debt is left to be paid. If the deceased person's estate is available, the debt is paid off from its proceeds. If that is not an option, the debt does not automatically get transferred to the family or friends, but it may if anyone takes that responsibility. In a way, this type of transfer of responsibility of a debt is encouraged to provide justice to the lending party, and a charity for the relatives, especially if they are resourceful. During the Prophet SAWs life, he encouraged this practice, and at one point offered his service, or assets, to cover for the debt of a deceased Muslim no one else paid.

Debt is also a common part of business. In case of a partnership, if it is being terminated and while settling its affairs, one is allowed and obligated to settle its debt. In this manner, one, two or all partners may inherit a debt commitment. The Prophet SAW also recommended to pay the debt on time, when it was due, without procrastination. He said that delayed payment of a debt by a rich person, or the one who could afford to pay it off, was injustice to the lender. When due and not paid, a lender is justified to demand for the lent amount, even in somewhat harsh or strong language. If a person died with a debt, it is paid before any other payment is made, including to the legal heirs. When paying back a loan, it is allowed to add an additional amount as a goodwill gesture. At the same time, compassion is recommended for someone who is having difficulty paying it off, and in worst case scenario, it is recommended to forgive the loan altogether as charity, which, as per the Quran, carries high regard with a bigger reward guaranteed by Allah SWT.

#22: The Concept of *Waqf* or Endowment

Though historically it is a much older concept, there is a strong tradition of endowment, or the *Waqf* in Islam. The Prophet SAW encouraged this activity, and at the end, donated almost all his resources in this manner. Many of his close associates did the same, and since then it became an eminent Islamic tradition. The founder of Pakistan, Muhammad Ali Jinnah, a reasonably wealthy man, donated all his assets in this manner. The oldest known university in the world is the University of Al-Karaouine, in the city of Fez, Morocco. It was established in the year 859 through a grant by a woman, Fatima al-Fihri, may Allah SWT be please with her, who used her inheritance to fund and sustain this project, initially a *masjid* and an adjacent *madrassa*.

Waqf or contributing to an endowment is a distinct type of charity. Instead of utilizing the donated amount right away, or the resources (such as estate, business, or financial assets), they are kept within a protected and usually permanent entity called a *waqf* or a trust. It may only be used by that institution, and sometimes only for a particular purpose. As a rule, for its long-term sustenance, it is best to only use a fraction of it every year, in current financial environment, not more than 2-3%. On top of that, due to inflation and the ever-expanding role of the benefiting institution, the endowed amount may require constant source of donations. This is true for the Harvard University in Boston, currently with the largest endowment in the world, or any smaller institution.

Waqf or the endowment may lead to significant permanent financial activity in a community. Beside fulfilling the basic purpose of its enterprise, it may provide permanent employment opportunities for people and its associated communal benefit. Contribution in a *Waqf* is not just for the rich, anyone may take part in it, even with modest resources. Technically, the value of a charity by someone making 10,000 a year and contributing 100, is 10 times higher than someone making a million and contributing 1,000. The Prophet SAW strongly recommended charity, with his words and personal example. One of his famous sayings was that (paraphrasing) "do charity, even if a single date."

Currently, the Islamic institutions in the USA, both local and on national levels, are in the process of building their endowments for long-term sustenance, and for the future generations of Muslims. Unfortunately, despite its strong Islamic traditions, for many, it is still a difficult concept to grasp. This is one of the limiting factors restricting expansion of much needed services at Islamic centers.

#23: The Laws of Inheritance

This subject is only briefly mentioned here, as part of it is an integral part of financial activities. Understanding the conflict-ridden nature of estate inheritance, many related specific measures are clearly mentioned in the Quran. In general, inheritance of the estate and its disposition to the legal heirs, as recommended in the Law, is obligatory. It is not allowed to withhold inheritance or to delay it, except in certain situations. For example, it is allowed to delay the legal transfer if the heirs are children, until they reach an appropriate age. Keeping with the spirit of responsibility and accountability, while transferring assets or compiling wills, we are asked to be careful and not give away the resources if the receiving child or the relative, or anyone else for that matter, is irresponsible or not wise, and may easily waste or lose them. At the same time, it is not allowed to take away anyone's legal rights in inheritance, including the one with mental incapacity (whose inheritance may be assigned to a guardian).

The concept of legal inheritance (the share ordained by Allah SWT in the Quran) is so strong in Islam that it may be confusing for a non-Muslim or even for a Muslim not fully versed with the letter and the spirit of Islam. Islam does not accept the typical argument that, "it is my money, I decide who to give it to." Allah SWT stated that all resources belong to Him, and we only have a temporary possession of it. He is the ultimate Inheritor. One may not, for example, take away his children (both sons and daughters) or anyone else's defined rights from

Chapter 14 – The Rules of Islamic Finance

his estate, even if they do not have good relations. We are only entrusted with the material resources we may control in our lifetime. We are asked to safeguard our possessions, use them in a manner recommended by Allah SWT and his Prophet SAW, and responsibly transfer the left-over to the next generation(s).

The Quran, Al-Nisa, *ayah* 5 (Al-Quran 4:5):

> "To those weak of understanding make not over your property which Allah hath made a means of support for you, but feed and clothe them therewith, and speak to them words of kindness and justice." Ali.

> "And give not unto the foolish your property which Allah has made a means of support for you, but feed and clothe them therewith, and speak to them words of kindness and justice." Al-Hilali & Khan.

Unlike a typical western or American tradition, Islamic laws of inheritance result in transfer of assets to the children, the spouse, parents, siblings, and even other related people. It is more of a charitable transfer instead of just a familial transfer of wealth.

The Quran, An-Nisa, ayah 33 (Al-Quran 4:33):

"To (benefit) everyone We have appointed sharers and heirs to property left by parents and relatives. To those also to whom your right hand was pledged give their due portion: For truly Allah is Witness to all things." Ali.

"And to everyone, We have appointed heirs of that (property) left by parents and relatives. To those also with whom you have made a pledge (brotherhood), give them their due portion (by Wasiyyah will). Truly, Allah is Ever a Witness over all things." Al-Halili & Khan.

Islamic system is a vehicle to provide potential support and sustenance to many who may not earn, like the parents, and to spread the wealth in the community instead of its control by a few. It is strongly recommended to have a living-will, especially if one is traveling, to avoid any potential conflicts that may arise. Also, it is recommended, if there are enough resources and not at the price of leaving the spouse, children (or the parents) with poverty, to bequeath part of the inheritance (not more than $1/3^{rd}$ of the estate) to charity. Finally, it shall be known that for the people living in a society without an Islamic system in place, the so-called "law of the land" may supersede, especially if a challenge is brought up by an heir.

#24: Prohibition of Non-refundable Advance Payment

In day-to-day business, there can be many situations where an advance payment may be required, especially if the product is too expensive or precious to obtain or produce. In some situations, it makes a better sense, like a farmer asking for an advance to grow a crop or raise cattle to be delivered in a year or a few years. It may be required to cover the material and labor cost. Its applications in many other sales are for a different purpose, such as advance payment on a routine real estate purchase (not for a home to be built), or to book an automobile to be purchased, whose primary purpose is to bind a customer to the sale. If the house or the car is not bought, the seller of the house or the auto-dealer may keep the advanced payment. This type of advance payment is disapproved by the Prophet SAW:

Sunan Abu Dawud, Vol. 4, Chapter 67, 3502: It was narrated from Malik bin Anas that it was conveyed to him that 'Amr bin Shuaib narrated from his father, that his grandfather said: "The Messenger of Allah SAW forbade non-refundable advances."

The logic of this statement may become clear to someone who understands that as per a different rule, if a contract is signed to make a trade, or buy something, the buyer is required to fulfill that commitment. At the same time, someone is not allowed to take money or a wage and not deliver any product or perform any service, if it is a clear violation of a different rule. This is the routine understanding, but in case of emergencies or some other reason, which can happen, the buyer may not be able to buy the product, or the seller may not be able to deliver it. In such situations, a just solution is advised, either through mutual negotiations or a legal arbitration.

#25: Conflict of Interest

Muslim societies struggle with this rule more often than many others. This may partly be due to lack of its proper understanding, especially it's wide scope and long-lasting negative impact. This rule is important when designing a system to prevent fraud and financial injustice, and in situations where arbitration is involved. The Quran provides its indirect basis:

The Quran, Al-Baqarah, *ayah* 282 (Al-Quran 2:282)

> "O ye who believe! When ye deal with each other, in transactions involving future obligations in a fixed period of time, reduce them to writing; let a scribe write down faithfully between the parties;

let not the scribe refuse to write: as Allah has taught him, so let him write. Let him who incurs the liability dictate. But let him fear his Lord Allah, and not diminish aught of what he owes. If the party liable is mentally deficient, or weak, or unable himself to dictate, let his guardian dictate faithfully. And get two witnesses, out of your own men, and if there are not two men, then a man and two women, such as ye choose, for witnesses, so that if one of them errs, the other can remind her. The witnesses should not refuse when they are called on (for evidence). Disdain not to reduce to writing (your contract) for a future period. Whether it be small or big: it is juster in the sight of Allah, more suitable as evidence, and more convenient to prevent doubts among yourselves but if it be a transaction which ye carry out on the spot among yourselves there is no blame on you if ye reduce it not to writing. But take witnesses whenever ye make a commercial contract; and let neither scribe nor witness suffer harm. If ye do (such harm), it would be wickedness in you. So fear Allah; for it is Allah that teaches you. And Allah is well acquainted with all things." Ali.

"O you who believe! When you contract a debt for a fixed period, write it down. Let a scribe write it down in justice between you. Let not the scribe refuse to write as Allah has taught him, so let him write. Let him (the debtor) who incurs the liability dictate, and he must fear Allah, his Lord, and diminish not anything of what he owes. But if the debtor is of poor understanding, or weak, or is unable himself to dictate, then let his guardian dictate in justice. And get two witnesses out of your own men. And if there are not two men (available), then a man and two women, such as you agree for witnesses, so that if one of them (two women) errs, the other can remind her. And the witnesses should not refuse when they are called on (for evidence). You should not become weary to write it (your contract), whether it be small or big, for its fixed term, that is more just with Allah; more solid as evidence, and more convenient to prevent doubts among yourselves, save when it is a present trade which you carry out on the spot among yourselves, then there is no sin on you if you do not write it down. But take witnesses whenever you make a commercial contract. Let neither scribe nor witness suffer any harm, but if you do (such harm), it would be wickedness in you. So be afraid of Allah; and Allah teaches you. And Allah is the All-Knower of each and everything." Al-Hilali and Khan.

In multiple ways, Allah SWT is asking us to take steps to avoid situation that may lead to deceit or even an impression of a deceit ("Let him who incurs the liability dictate," "if the debtor is of poor understanding, or weak, or is unable himself to dictate, then let his guardian dictate in justice," "get witnesses,"). All these are examples of ways of avoiding conflict-of-interest in financial transactions.

In other examples in the Quran, we are asked to involve a representative from each side when trying to resolve differences between a husband and a wife:

The Quran, An-Nisa, ayah 35 (Al-Quran 4:35):

> "If ye fear a breach between them twain, appoint (two) arbiters, one from his family and the other from her's; if they wish for peace, Allah will cause their reconciliation: for Allah hath full knowledge, and is acquainted with all things" Ali.

> "If you fear a breach between them twain (the man and his wife), appoint (two) arbitrators, one from his family and the other from her's if they both wish for peace, Allah will cause their reconciliation. Indeed Allah is Every All-Knower, Well-Acquainted with all things." Al-Hilali & Khan.

We are asked to do justice and provide truthful testimony even if it is against our own interests. A more practical example was when Omar RA reprimanded a Zakat collector when he claimed that something given to him in his official capacity belonged to him, claiming that it was a gift given to him. This rule is critical for proper corporate governance, which is discussed in a later chapter.

CHAPTER 15

ISLAMIC FINANCE IN REAL LIFE, OR ITS PRACTICAL IMPLICATIONS

With constantly evolving human society, real life situations may continue to change and become less predictable. In a social or a political system, agreeing with generally established principles and rules, is a necessary first step. As the basic purpose of finance is to earn money or resources, people are constantly inclined to find newer ways to outmaneuver each other. While it is not uncommon to hear the cliché that Islam provides solution for all the situations, all the time; it is important to point out that Muslim societies of thousand years have failed to provide a financial model to match that claim. In my opinion, one of the reasons for that problem is the notion that anything originating in a non-Muslim, or a competing financially successful society, is inherently un-Islamic. Instead of judging a product on its merit, which requires a formal critical analysis based upon pertinent rules and regulations, people frequently rely on summary judgments. On the other hand, there is over-emphasis on creating "Islamic" finance, bank, or a mortgage system, whose difference from the mainstream at times is more in semantics than in substance. In this chapter I discuss different aspects of a financial system, and their status in relation to Islamic business regulations. Where possible, suggestions are provided to modify the system to fulfill or meet the Islamic standards.

The Capital

According to Islamic principles, all resources of every kind ultimately belong to the Creator, Allah SWT, the Owner of everything created.

Al-Quran, Al-Baqarah, *ayah* 284 (Al-Quran 2:284)

> "To Allah belongeth all that is in the heavens and on earth." Ali.

> " To Allah belongs all that is in the heavens and all that is on the earth," Al-Hilali & Khan.

Human ownership is always transient and is rather considered a trust or temporary custody of assets, which may end anytime in life, or ultimately with death. We are told to be mindful of this trust, not be pompous, and avoid wasting wealth and resources. As more and more assets are assigned to a person, higher becomes their responsibility:

Al-Quran, Al-Anam, *ayah* 165 (Al-Quran 6:165):

> "It is He Who hath made you (His) agents, inheritors of the earth: He hath raised you in ranks,

Chapter 15 – Islamic Finance in Real Life, or its Practical Implications

some above others: that He may try you in the gifts He hath given you:" Ali.

"And it is He Who has made generations coming after generations, replacing each other on the earth. And He has raised you in ranks, some above others that He may try you in that which He has bestowed on you." Al-Hilali & Khan.

Al-Quran, Al-Hijr, *ayah* 23 (Al-Quran 15:23)
"And verily, it is We Who give life, and Who give death: it is We Who remain Inheritors (after all else passes away)." Ali.

"And certainly We! We it is Who give life, and cause death, and We are the Inheritors." Al-Hilali & Khan.

On the other hand, personal proprietorship or ownership is deeply respected, and considered a sacred trust. One is allowed to fight defending his or her interests, and assets. Trading or business, in an open-market system, is the way when resources circulate and, in a way, share by the larger society. As referenced above, Islam encourages and promotes trade or business. But not everyone is resourceful, and some ventures require too large of a resource for a person or a few people to finance.

In a situation where resources are needed to start or run a business, Islam does not specify what to do but rather what not to do. One option is to borrow money and return it without any extra charge, the so-called *qard e hasanah* or interest-free loan, without any other arrangement. This type of transaction, on one hand is allowed, and encouraged, but has limited use. *Qard e hasanah* based transactions may be useful and applicable for small private or charitable loans but are not a practical model for business, especially large-scale business. This model is also impractical to solve some common and intractable societal issues, such as housing for the larger population. This is because in charitable and personal loans, the primary motive for the lender is to help someone, or charity. On the other hand, the primary motive of an investor in a business transaction is to earn or make more money. Businesses or investors are not interested in lending or investing money without any benefit to them, which to them make a logical business sense. There is no large-scale example one can provide of a society, where businesses flourished, or large-scale societal issues are resolved, using a *qard e hasanah* model of lending. This cannot be done by a government either, as the money owned or controlled by the government, like a business, ultimately belonged to the people. The capital or the resources are seldom free of cost.

Islam accepts and respects financial ownership, to the extent that, unlike a Western model, both husband and wife, or men and women, are free to maintain a separate financial estate.

The Quran, An-Nisa, ayah 32 (Al-Quran 4:32):

> "And in no wise covet those things in which Allah hath bestowed His gifts more freely on some of you than on others; to men is allowed what they earn, and to women what they earn: but ask Allah of His bounty: for Allah hath full knowledge of all things." Ali.

Chapter 15 – Islamic Finance in Real Life, or its Practical Implications

"And wish not for the things in which Allah has made some of you to excel others. For men there is reward for what they have earned, (and likewise) for women there is reward for that they have earned, and ask Allah of His Bounty. Surely, Allah is Ever All-Knower of everything." Al-Hilali & Khan.

In general, the state or the ruler may not acquire or subvert their assets or capital, a concept radically different from the abusive tribal or monarchial, and the unjust or unnatural communist systems. Using their capital, people are free to invest, trade, and prosper, as much as they like, though moderation is encouraged. They are also free to join hands, in partnerships, and benefit each other or take larger projects. What is not allowed and strongly discouraged is stealing, begging, wasting resources, or taking loans one may not afford or pay off. Personal responsibility and accountability in all matters, including finance, are some of the fundamental Islamic principles.

In an Islamic system business capital is private and public owned, in contrast to government owned, resulting in promotion of private enterprises, the hallmark of a successful financial system. If we review the financial situation of a typical Islamic country of today, like Pakistan or Egypt, one may not ignore the pitfalls of government ownership with its officials, civil or military, overseeing businesses. Instead of benefiting the whole society, or leading to universal prosperity, the so-called government or semi-government system of business creates wealth for the select group of connected people, civil and military officials, their families and friends. Though the capital that established those businesses ultimately came from the public, the tax money, or the natural resources, it benefits mostly a few, which is manifest injustice, a gross violation of Islamic principles. People benefiting from this biased and unjust way of business, routinely justify their practices with claims about the wrongs of the "capitalist" system while ignoring their own offenses. Also, on one hand, it seems attractive to use tax-based capital for business ventures, any such system is always at risk of political maneuvering and cronyism. It is highly unlikely that these practices can lead to financial prosperity for the whole society, and without undoing these structural injustices, blessings of Allah SWT may not be expected.

Historically speaking, in the Muslim societies of the past where Islamic jurisprudence was in operation, businesspeople and/or scholars, like the Islamic financial experts of contemporary era, came up with a variety of arrangements that allowed people to get the necessary resources for business while avoiding what was forbidden. For example, in one arrangement the lender, instead of just lending the money (and by doing so merely dealing with the money) became a partner in the business, sharing both profits and losses. The terms of the contract were negotiated between the lender and the borrower, and the whole process was governed and supervised, directly or indirectly, by a supervising authority whose job was to make sure that appropriate rules were followed, and no injustice took place. In recent times, partly due to a relatively limited role of "Muslim" governments in Islamic business transactions, the so-called Sharia Compliance Boards have taken a part of this responsibility.

The key to financial prosperity for a society is to promote, protect, and troubleshoot private enterprise. The job of the government, both civil and military, is not to start or run businesses; government's role is the governance. At the same time, if it is acceptable to the general public and does not violate any basic Islamic principles, there may be allowance for the government to take over some large-scale civil projects, like the roads, bridges, and dams, which benefit the society at large, has a larger purpose more than just making money, and may not be an attractive or practical business venture, both for businessman and the government. While doing that, it is important to follow Islamic guidelines of responsibility and accountability, and to avoid injustice and cronyism. Where needed, there are ways, without breaking any Islamic rules, to raise large-scale funds to foster private enterprise. This issue is further elaborated under discussion about financial bonds. Numerous countries have been ruined or are in deep financial predicament due to inappropriate borrowing, corruption, and waste. The national debt created in this manner, is a financial burden for their generations to come.

The Banks

The concept of a bank did not exist centuries ago, but in present—day systems, a society without a bank is fathomable but not practical. All modern consumer or commercial banks follow similar rules. To establish a bank, one needs some base capital, and a system where people may safely and reliably deposit and withdraw their money.

Islam promotes trade or business and forbids *Riba*. Lending money for certain duration, without taking part in the venture and/or bearing the risk of loss and expecting a pre-determined higher or unreasonable amount in return, by an individual or an institution without any other financial arrangement, is forbidden in Islam. This is the classic *Riba*, because there is *dharar* to one party (the borrower) over the other, and the transaction carries significant uncertainty or *gharar* (for the lender). Banks earned money mostly by lending and charging fixed or variable surcharge on the money they lent, which is generally considered the classic *Riba*, or *Riba* by deferment. They are not in the business of starting or partnering a business venture, meaning that they do not make money by selling any material product, or establishing businesses. Bank(s) may be indirectly involved in these activities.

Scholars have somewhat struggled with the relationship between the depositor of an account and the bank. The main purpose of an account is to safeguard and manage one's wealth, not loaning to the bank, as keeping it with oneself or at home is neither practical nor safe. The bank provides a service to its customers to safeguard their money. In doing so, it is justified to charge a price for the service, if it decides to do so. Money is also a fungible item, with an implication that the money obtained from the bank by a customer is not the same money that was deposited.

The other issue with banking is the "interest" banks offer to its customers on saving account, or the account held for a certain time-period. Some scholars have differed from mainstream impression that any money that a bank pays to its depositors in this manner is illegal and is under the category of forbidden *Riba*. Here and there, there has been disagreement, some of it in respected circles. Following is an example of such an opinion:

Chapter 15 – Islamic Finance in Real Life, or its Practical Implications

Opinion on Certain Interest on Bank Accounts

- **(Shaykh-ul-Azhar) Dr. Muhammad Sayyid Tantawi:** (paraphrased) Not all fixed interest on bank account is *haram* if the terms are clear, they are mutually agreeable, not harmful to either party over other (bank or the depositor) and is beneficial to both parties. In the Quran, *Hadith* or the *Seerah* it is neither explicitly permitted nor explicitly forbidden and does not belong to the domains of creeds or formal acts of worship, wherein change or alteration is not allowed.

One may understand the logic of this opinion by comparing it to the one in Al-Muwatta:

> "Usury in the *jahiliyya* was that a man would give a loan to a man for a set term. When the term was due, he would say, 'Will you pay it off or increase me?' If the man paid, he took it. If not, he increased him in his debt and lengthened the term for him."

Though most Muslim scholars rejected Dr. Tantawi's opinion, it is difficult to disregard his reasoning. It is important to understand that not every additional amount paid back to the lender is *Riba*, and the payment of an additional amount is not its exclusively essential characteristics. If this was the definition of *Riba*, one may have difficulty explaining other situations described in *Hadith*, where no additional amount was involved, but they were clearly described as *Riba* (explained in detail in a previous chapter). With that understanding, one may notice that there is a difference between these two transactions, one described in Al-Muwatta, and the other by Dr. Tantawi. In the former transaction, terms of the transaction were not clear, they were not pre-arranged, were arbitrary, and with almost no control for the borrower. This led to an arrangement mostly beneficial to the lender, and frequently abusive to the borrower, both situations clearly in conflict with the basic rules of Islamic finance.

Depositor-Banker Relationship

Another aspect to explore is the depositor-banker relationship: Is it a business relationship? Is a bank justified to charge a fee on deposits? Can the money deposited in the bank be declared an investment? Shall the depositor be paid a part of the income generated by the bank using the depositor's money?

The following example may help to understand this issue: Money is a fungible item, like any grain, or precious metal. The matter of non-fungible items is straightforward; banks routinely charge a fee to safeguard any precious item, like documents or jewelry. Let's say, we are depositing wheat instead of money in a bank. We can easily understand the difficulties a bank may have to keep and safeguard the grain. Instead, the bank may sell most of it, and keep a small amount to accommodate if someone wants to withdraw. One may also understand that the bank is justified to charge a fee for that service. The function of a bank is to provide guarantee that the same amount of similar fungible item, money or the grain, can always be withdrawn, with a fair notice.

Even though banks are indirectly involved in business with the depositor's money, the depositors have not agreed to bear any loss to their deposits, and so may not justifiably expect full part of the profit. A Muslim depositor or an investor must make sure that the bank does not violate any Islamic rules of conduct and finance. Otherwise, he or she may become a part of an unjust or un-Islamic enterprise. The issue of the unrealistic or irrational risk taken by banks, with their depositor's money, by getting involved in inherently risky ventures (e. g., derivatives or securities trading) is also noted by the regulators, and an effort is made for its control. An Islamic bank must be fully controlled to avoid any such risky activity.

Investment Banking

Part of banking is the so-called investment banking, which is somewhat a different type of business. While the primary function of commercial banking is to maintain personal and business deposit accounts, the primary function of investment banking is to help individuals profit from their investments, and businesses and institutions to establish new ventures, especially on the larger scale. Because of the size of investments, and less rigid regulations in comparison to the commercial banking, investment banks frequently deal with high-risk/high-reward schemes, which when fail can be detrimental to the larger society. The primary mode of income for commercial banks is either the fee for their services, or the extra charge on the money they lend. Investment banks primarily profit from the fee (in terms of percentages) charged for investments, or business ventures. Because of the regulations in place, neither of these banks is allowed to assume any direct role in business ventures.

The Islamic Finance and the Riba

If any amount of interest a bank charges for a loan is declared *Riba*, which is one of the main, or the main, instrument for commercial banks to make profit, this type of banking model may not be approved in Islam. In that case, everyone facilitating this activity, working in or for the bank, becomes liable for his or her actions. Investment banking is somewhat more complicated, and some of its activity, like commercial banking, can be laden with *Riba*, and may not be approved. Another large part of its business, e.g., help establishing new public companies, does not seem to have any specific Islamic restriction.

Human society is in evolution, and in general, trying to make it ever more just. But the tendency and practice to do wrong has not abated either. Even in a financially sophisticated society like the USA, some aspects of lending have not much changed in centuries. Many companies exploit borrower's needs with excessive amount of surcharge, disproportionate amount of fees, or easy seizure of basic-need collaterals, like the automobile. The society, through some conscientious politicians, continues to try mitigating these ills, only to be stopped by self-serving many others. Lending and borrowing are not all the same, there are tremendous variations, some extremely exploitative, and many relatively just. May be, in every example, one must look at the detail before giving a final judgment. See comparison of two types of loans provide as an example on next page.

Chapter 15 – Islamic Finance in Real Life, or its Practical Implications

	Type A	Type B
A loan was given for an agreed upon time	Yes	Yes
Collateral	Usually yes. It was unlikely to get a loan without collateral or having definable assets that could pay off the loan	Defined collateral, assets that could pay off the loan, or some other proof (like an appropriately paid job) of affordability
If the loan was returned at agreed upon time	Usually, no extra charge	The same
If the loan was not returned at agreed upon time	Extra charge based upon an arbitrary rate of return, usually quite high, especially its increment	Extra charge based upon an agreed rate of return, which was based upon a market standard, and not arbitrary
If the debtor was unable to pay and defaulted on a loan	The lender was free to acquire any of debtor's property or assets. In worse case, abduction, enslavement or physical harm was not uncommon	The lender could not touch debtor's personal property (other than collateral) or household items, and could not do any physical harm
If the debtor died before paying off the debt	The debt was paid from debtor's estate, and any unpaid debt was transferred to the children or the family, including all extra higher-than-normal charges, many times enslaving generations of the original borrower	The debt was paid from debtor's estate, and any unpaid debt was written off. It did not get transferred to the children or the family
Supervising body	None, or minimal (e.g., tribal elders) or without full legal supervision and protection	Full legal supervision and protection
Benefit to a party	Lender's benefit outweighed the borrower's	Either same, or the borrower profited more (by fulfilling his or her need) than the lender
Harm to a party (Dharar)	Could be to either, but the risk to the borrower was much higher. Many borrowers were financially ruined, or physically enslaved	Equal to both or none to both
Uncertainty factor (Gharar)	Frequently significant due to lack of oversight, and abusive practices, and more for the borrower than the lender	Smaller, in "fine-print", controlled by the rules in place

The Comparison of Two Types of Loans

One may see from this comparison that loans may differ in some critical manner. They can vary in terms of financial injustice they may inflict, some with more and some others with minimal or none. After reviewing this, one may understand the rationale for the opinion provided by Dr. Tantawi, may Allah SWT forgive his shortcomings. A better course of action for Muslim societies (both in Muslim and non-Muslim countries) is to review this subject closely, and for their own interests, promote even more just (both to the borrower and the lender), and merciful financial lending practices.

The Home Financing

Home financing is one of the major areas where many people deal with the issue of money lending. A common model for home financing is the so-called conventional mortgage. This does not involve an open-ended or unrestricted borrowing, and to understand the difference one shall critically review its different aspects. The difference of opinion on this subject, within the scholars, is partly due to its critical difference from a conventional or open-ended loan. The money contributed or lent by the bank is never in possession of the buyer of the house, and it is never meant to be for any other use (the home equity loan is a separate entity). Before going into further details, following is the snapshot of some of the opinions on this subject.

Opinions on Conventional Home Mortgage

- **Most common or the default opinion:** The interest a bank charges to buy a home is the forbidden *Riba*, and so the conventional mortgaging is not allowed.

- **Muhammad Tahir ul Qadri**: Mortgaging for Muslims in Canada, US, and UK is "permissible due to exceptional circumstances."

- **Javed Ahmad Ghamadi**: Mortgaging is allowed. The so-called interest is the same additional money that otherwise is called profit. *Riba* rule do not apply when buying an item like a house or a car; it applies for fungible items like money, grain, and similar exchangeable things. What we call interest is equal to the rental money for the house.

- **Shaykh Atabek Shukurov an Nasafi**: It is not haram based upon principles of *Hanafi fiqh*. The loan for home is not a debt as per Islamic principles; the person getting it never really possess it. It is not a *Qard* as in Islam and the additional amount or interest on it is not the usury or the forbidden *Riba*.

- **Al-Sayyid Ali Al-Sistani**: For Muslims living in non-Muslim countries, conventional mortgage is allowed, if you make an intention of not getting the money as a "loan."

- **Yusuf Al-Qaradawi:** Conventional mortgage in non-Muslim lands is allowed based upon, 1. The opinion of Imam Abu Hanifa, RA who allowed *Riba* in non-Muslim lands, 2. Determination that the mortgager is the primary beneficiary from mortgage home financing, and 3. Invoking the rule of necessity.

- **Dr. Muzammil H. Siddiqi** explaining the *Fiqh* Council of North America approach: If a person is not able to rent a suitable house at a proper location or the rent is too high, he/she may use conventional mortgage. It may also be done, instead of paying interest, by making an arrangement with the seller to sell him the house at a higher price, and he pays it in installments.

Despite an impression that some of these views seems tenuous, one may not just ignore them. Each scholar has used an apparently viable justification. I note that many scholars spent much of the discussion about this topic to state that people do not need to buy houses; they may reside in rental properties. The issue of renting or not renting is not relevant to this discussion and is a matter of choice, which is made due to number of factors unique to every individual, including availability, affordability, and the duration of stay in a particular place.

After reading these and other views about this subject, I summarize them as follows:

View #1: Conventional home mortgaging is illegal in Islam, without exception. This point of view does not accept the notion that there may be variance in lending, some just and others unjust, or the fact that the nature of home mortgaging is different from a conventional loan. For believers of this point of view, any pre-negotiated extra amount is the forbidden *Riba*, which is not allowed, making it illegal.

View #2: Conventional home mortgaging is illegal in Islam, but an exception can be made in non-Islamic societies, due to the logic of necessity and/or undue burden, to make it permissible.

View #3: Home mortgaging is not a typical loan. In a typical home-mortgage transaction, despite what city records may state, the house is neither completely owned by the owner, or the bank. The ownership is mutual, until the part bank contributes is paid off. The bank never allows full utilization of buyer's ownership without getting the part it contributes. Secondly, the buyer never takes possession of the money that the bank pays to the seller. The bank pays the money to the seller, and in exchange puts a lien on the house to maintain its part of the ownership. The person living in it gets the whole house, partly on credit. As house is not a fungible item like grain or money, an additional agreed-upon amount paid to the bank is justified. A conventional bank calls this additional amount the interest, and the Islamic bank labels it the profit, or the rent, depending upon how the deal is structured. In both cases, the additional amount is decided based upon market conditions, not arbitrarily, and the government provided financial benchmarks. It is not decided based upon any projections about the future value of the house, which may be less or more than it is bought for. *Riba* rules do not apply to this transaction because, a. they are applicable to fungible items (money is fungible, but it is not an open-ended amount given to the buyer; and it is the house the buyer is given possession of, not the money), and b. the extra amount or the "interest" is akin to the profit on investment, or the rent on property. It is fair to the lender for its investment in the house, and beneficial to the person owning the house. Any amount of *dharar* or *gharar i*s eliminated or minimized with better lending practices laws, which protect interests of the investor, the buyer of the house, and the society at large.

What about Islamic Mortgage?

As stated above, the most accepted point of view about the conventional mortgage, especially by the religious leadership, living in non-Muslim societies is the first one, that conventional mortgage involved *Riba*, and it is not allowed. This creates a problem for those who do not want to be involved in a major sin, the *Riba*, resulting in a market vacuum. The solution available to them is the so-called Islamic mortgage, or Islamic financing. Is Islamic mortgage different from the conventional mortgage? If it is, how is it different? These are fair questions for any discerning customer.

The following table (next pages) provides comparison of two systems of mortgaging, the conventional versus the so-called Islamic, as practiced in the West:

Chapter 15 – Islamic Finance in Real Life, or its Practical Implications

Comparison of Conventional Mortgage and "Islamic" Mortgage

	Conventional Mortgage	"Islamic" Mortgage
House search and selection	Done by the borrower	The same
Creditworthiness, or the ability to buy the house	Checked by using standard financial instruments, including credit scoring	The same
Down payment from the borrower	Usually required, sometimes up to 20% or more, in most cases less than 5%, depending upon creditworthiness	Almost always required, and typically higher than the conventional banks, depending upon creditworthiness
Who paid most of the money to the seller?	Usually, the bank or an intermediary institution	The same
Did a buyer ever get hold of the money from the bank paid to the seller?	No	The same
Who owned the house then?	On paper, the borrower, but not completely or with limited control until the loan was paid off	Either the same, or an intermediary trust created for this purpose, which guaranteed similar controlling stakes for the financing institution until the money financed was fully paid
Did the bank own the house before it was sold to the borrower?	In most cases, no.	It might. To fulfill an "Islamic" criterion, the bank might take momentary ownership, during the documents signing process, before selling it to the borrower. Or it was done by an intermediary trust. In both cases the bank's stakes in the property were guaranteed, as much as it contributed for the transaction.
How did the bank safeguard its investment?	Lien on the title of the house, as technically bank was the partial owner until the loan was paid off	The same
What parameters were used to calculate extra charge?	a. Market situation b. Government control – central banking rates	The same
What if the borrower defaulted?	After a grace period, and sometimes negotiations, the bank might acquire the house, to sell and get its money back.	The same

The Islamic Finance and the Riba

Who was the primary beneficiary?	The borrower – if done right	The same
What benefit the bank had?	A: Ability to invest money in fixed asset, the house, and its earning	A: The same
	B: Agreed upon charge based upon market price, not an arbitrary number – it was called interest	B: Agreed upon charge based upon market price, not an arbitrary number – it was called profit or rent or mark-up
What benefit the borrower had?	Ability to live in a house not completely owned, and the option to own it by paying it off in installments	The same
What was the risk for the bank?	The borrower might stop paying, which could create a significant problem for the bank. The bank could reclaim its investment, but the process was difficult, cumbersome, expensive, and seldom beneficial	The same
What was the risk for the borrower?	Not much. The borrower might lose the ability to make monthly payments. But even then, his or her equity in the house remained intact	The same
What if the house gained in value, who got the benefit?	The borrower	The same
What if the house lost its value, who bore the loss?	The borrower, if he or she was able to afford it	The same
	The lender, if the borrower was not able to afford to pay back the amount bank contributed	
Who lost, if the borrower was unable to make payments?	In financial terms, the lender.	The same
	The borrower might lose his/her reputation or creditworthiness (even that for a limited time)	

One may ascertain that there hardly is any difference, and if there is one, it is more in semantics than in substance. Islamic banks call the extra charge on the money they contribute, "profit or mark-up", while emphasizing that it is not, "interest." Though, there hardly is any difference at all between the two. Both amounts are calculated using the same measures and tools, added to the principal amount, and amortized. In case the client is a non-Muslim, he or she may not notice any difference at all, except that the Islamic financial institutions are usually more expensive. For a Muslim client, it creates a guilt-free feeling, like entering a *Halal* restaurant. Hardly anyone ever questions or investigates the restaurant's claim, if the food is really *tayyab* and *halal*, and how is that achieved and maintained.

Extending the analogy of *halal* and *tayyab* meat, someone may use an argument that in technical terms (i.e., how an animal is killed and butchered) may exactly be the same but even then, if it is not killed with the right intention and statements, it is not allowed to be consumed. Similarly, even if the details of financial transactions (between a conventional and an "Islamic" mortgage) seem the same, one is allowed and the other not. But this type of comparison is problematic: In case of killing and eating an animal, the significance and impact of the action and its intention is an issue between Allah SWT and an individual. On the other hand, financial matters like mortgage involve other people, with its direct impact, *dharar*, over one to the other.

Let's look at this issue in a different and more practical manner. In the following table, are two searches I just did on the net, for a loan of $100,000 to be used to buy a house. The first column provides the numbers from IjaraCDC, which is a business in Ann Arbor, Michigan, offering Islamic Financial Alternative. The second column carries the numbers provided by the Google loan calculator (the conventional loan):

The Islamic Finance and the Riba

	Ijara CDC	Google calculator
Description of loan	Ijara finance amount	Amount financed
Amount	100,000	100,000
Term	30 years (360 months)	30 years (360 months)
Monthly payment	536.82	537
Total cost	193,255.78	193,256
Additional amount	93,255.78	93,256
Label for the additional amount	Rent	Interest

If the concept of *Riba* is based solely upon the additional amount charged, both above transactions are charging almost equal amount. They are merely labeling it differently, interest versus rent. This example of a loan where an additional amount is expected in return, and the second type of *Riba* as defined in a previous chapter, in which there is no extra amount involved (in example of bartering dates of inferior quality with dates of higher quality), are enough to understand the reasons for difficulties Muslims always have gone through, even within the first generations, while defining the concept of *Riba*.

A financial transaction ought to follow all the rules and regulations described above, as not following even one of them may make it unjust and illegal. To designate a transaction as a *Riba* transaction, which is so strongly outlawed by the Quran and the *Hadith*, one may have to be extra careful and prove that rules are broken, beyond reasonable doubt. The final opinion shall be based upon any violation of rules and regulations, instead of merely stating that any additional amount is *Riba*, while it is abundantly clear that a *Riba* transaction may not involve any additional amount at all.

Chapter 15 – Islamic Finance in Real Life, or its Practical Implications

Is Any Additional Amount Paid to the Lender *Riba*?

The straight answer is no. If it is done as a gift or a goodwill gesture, it is explicitly allowed.

> Sahih Muslim, Vol. 4, 4111: It was narrated that Abu Hurairah said: "The Messenger of Allah SWT borrowed a camel, and gave back a camel that was better than it, and he said: 'The best of you are those who are the best in paying off debts.'"

> Sahih Al-Bukhari, Vol. 3, 2394: Narrated Jabir bin Abdullah RA: I went to the Prophet SAW while he was in the mosque. The Prophet SAW told me to offer two *Rakat* prayer, and then he repaid me the debt he owed me and gave me an extra amount.

There are two different ways to reflect and learn from these examples:

a. An additional amount on a loan is encouraged, but *only* allowed if given as a gift, as goodwill, or with pleasure, or

b. An additional amount on a loan is allowed, if it did not break any other rules of Islamic finance.

One shall also be careful about situations where the presumed difference between one and the other type of transaction may be the choice of words or a different label, without any significant material or structural distinction. For example, the following three paragraphs are copied from IjaraCDC (a business providing Islamic finance), which describe the arrangement of a sale. Other than putting different labels, the arrangement is pretty much the same as in any conventional mortgage:

> "You enter a partnership arrangement with a co-owner and sign a contract that specifies the terms of your agreement. After you find the home you want, you get approval to move ahead, and make an offer. Your partner or co-owner, usually a professional investment company rather than an individual, provides the lion's share of the purchase price. As part of the partnership agreement, you agree to make monthly payments to the partnership for your use of the home as **either explicit or implicit rent**. At the same time, you make regularly scheduled investments in the partnership to increase your equity, or ownership share, of the home. With each payment, the balance you owe the partnership declines, and your equity increases.
>
> The amount of your monthly payment is determined at the time of purchase, based on several factors including the price of the home, your credit rating, the amount of your initial payment, the term of the contract, and the current and projected fair market value of similar homes in the community where you buy."

The designation of a "partner" or "co-owner" for the financing entity (an individual or an institution like a bank) described above, in practical terms (i.e., legal rights and responsibilities), is no different from a conventional mortgage. As far as what is stated in the last paragraph, the projected payment plan, as exemplified above, is hardly any different.

Chapter 15 – Islamic Finance in Real Life, or its Practical Implications

Who Owns the Property Before it is Fully Paid off?

In the example of an Islamic home financing provided above, the IjaraCDC, the house is "owned" by a trust created for this purpose. The buyer of the house is assured of its benefit through legal protection, while the bank or an "investor" is guaranteed the value of its investment, and an additional mark-up in the form of "rental" payments, by acting as the trustee. In purely financial terms, this arrangement is a little complicated but not much different from a conventional mortgage; both the buyer and the bank are guaranteed the nature and extent of their agreed-upon share: the bank is guaranteed of at least the amount it invests, and the buyer is guaranteed the full ownership of the house, after the amount the bank contributes is paid off. So, in terms of guarantees for both parties, there is no difference between this and the so-called conventional mortgage.

The terminology used in the Islamic finance is of an "investor" instead of a lender or a bank, but in practical terms there hardly is any difference. In both cases, someone or an entity (an individual or a bank) is contributing the larger sum of money to purchase the house, acting as an investor. In both cases, a pre-negotiated return on investment is guaranteed. But this relationship of the investor with the buyer of the house is distinct in two important aspects: First, if the value of the house increased during the term of the deal, its benefit belongs only to the buyer. This happened in most cases, and the investor or the bank do not gain any additional benefit, more than the pre-negotiated amount on the investment. Second, sometimes, especially in a shorter term, the house may lose its value, in which case, the loss is also of the buyer. In the case of conventional mortgage, the

— 213

process is easy to explain, while in the Islamic financial arrangement, it happens in a bit complicated manner, which is usually difficult to understand for most customers, through an intermediary trust. This is explained as follows by IjaraCDC:

> "In compliance with Sharia law forbidding unequally shared risk *(Dharar)*, the trust is the sole owner and thus takes on 100% of the loss or gain, which it then passes along to the beneficiary, who is usually the customer."

Laws are in place to safeguard any additional damage (financial, physical, or even emotional) to the buyer, more than the amount contributed by the bank. In worst-case situations, where the buyer lacks any means to pay back the amount, depending upon overall financial situation, he or she can either walk away or declare bankruptcy. In the former case, the bank may be able to retrieve the money it contributes by selling the house, and in the later, it may just be forgiven. In case of bankruptcy, it is a business loss to the bank. If it happens on a larger scale, e.g., during deep recession, the loss is taken by the government, a charity from the taxpayers, not unlike the concept recommended by the Prophet SAW in such situations. To mitigate this issue, in both cases (for pure financial reasons for a conventional bank, and for *sharia* compliance reason for an Islamic bank), there is the option of a variable rate of "interest" or "rent," but that may make the deal too unpredictable and much less attractive for the buyer.

"Rent-on-Money" Versus "Rent-on-Property"

Companies try different ways to separate their way of business from the "conventional" mortgage. Some people use the above terms to differentiate the Islamic financing from a conventional mortgage stating that a conventional bank is charging "rent on money," while the Islamic bank is charging the "rent on property." It is not as black and white as it seemed, due to the reasons described above, and is more of a marketing gimmick and word play than a realistic representation. A different such example is the following I found on the net, about the description of home financing in Saudi Arabia:

> "Bank finance in Saudi Arabia must be compliant with Sharia law, which means interest isn't charged in a traditional sense. Instead, you make repayments on both the principal part of the loan and the 'rental' part – the part of the home owned by the bank."

And then there is this impression that one cannot just make money out of money without being part of a business or trade. This notion is also debatable due to the fact that the Prophet SAW clearly allowed hand-to-hand money-exchange, which by itself is also a valid business. A money exchanger is making money, its profit margin, by just having and exchanging it to a different currency, instead of taking part in any other business or type of trade.

At the end, every individual must decide by themselves. Enough information is available to make that decision. For someone who wants to rely on a scholar's opinion, a variety of opinions is available. For a more discerning individual, a lot more detail is provided. This economic issue has tremendous implications on societal level. Lack of a reliable system of home finance is the critical factor limiting home ownership in many societies, which indirectly impacts their generational wealth. Muslims are dealing with an additional layer of complication of finding ways to avoid what is prohibited in Islam. Any level of ease in this regard carries widespread economic significance with its multiple benefits to individuals and the society.

Checking and Saving Accounts

As stated above, it is possible but impractical and unsafe to have personal possession of any significant amount of money. One needs to put it somewhere for safekeeping and management. A bank provides this service, and as alluded above, there is no prohibition against opening an account with it. Bank accounts in general are of two types: Checking and a saving type. As money is a fungible item, banks are not required to keep the same money, or the currency notes a customer deposits. As establishing a reliable and safe banking institution is a complicated affair, a fee for accounts is justified, if the bank is inclined to charge one. To alleviate depositor's anxiety or a real risk of a loss, the Federal government in USA insures every bank account up to $250,000. This is good so far, except that the banks do not just hold the money, they invest it in other businesses.

Banks in the USA, and probably in most places, are barred from directly establishing or partnering in a business. This policy is considered beneficial to the society, because if that is allowed, banks will have unusually large control on the economy, much larger than what they may already have, which if not managed well may be detrimental to everyone.

Banks' involvement in business is indirect, through providing the resources for business, but with a price. They

Chapter 15 – Islamic Finance in Real Life, or its Practical Implications

charge a negotiated surcharge or interest on loans. Laws are in place to safeguard both the bank and the borrower's interests. One may argue, as elaborated above, that this kind of lending and borrowing is different from an abusive ancient system. If we understand that any amount of additional surcharge on a loan is the forbidden *Riba*, large part of banking business can be considered un-Islamic, in which case, the interest earned from deposits is not allowed. If on the other hand, we are flexible to consider the possibility that lending and borrowing can be tweaked in a way to eliminate any injustice to the bank and the borrower, there may be a way for the depositors to share in the bank's businesses. In one way or other, on academic level or in practice, Muslim societies are struggling to straighten a way out.

What About Stocks?

Following is a definition of a stock on the net: "A stock (also known as equity) is a security that represents the ownership of a fraction of a corporation. This entitles the owner of the stock to a proportion of the corporation's assets and profits, equal to the amount of stock they own. Units of stock are called "shares."" This arrangement does not break any Islamic law of finance or ethics, and is beneficial to the corporation, the stockholder, and the society. With fair chance of a profit or a loss, stocks provide an opportunity for anyone to benefit from businesses otherwise inaccessible to invest.

The stock option is an excellent tool for new ventures or businesses to open and thrive. It provides an option to raise capital to start or establish a business, and in return, it offers a part of ownership in the business. All stockholders, small or large, share in the company or business's profit and loss. There is no guarantee of profit or additional amount on investment. Stocks are routinely traded for short-term profit and loss, but their real value may be is for the long-term investors.

What about Bonds?

As we noted above, the main purpose of establishing stocks for a company is to raise capital at the start of a business. Sometimes, businesses or other agencies (municipalities or governments) also need to raise capital, to undertake larger expensive projects. As alluded above, interest-free lending does not help in real world or for big projects. The projects needing to establish bonds are so big that even local banks may not provide enough capital. A bond is basically a promissory note for certain duration, by a business or a government, of paying back its face value, and a fixed amount of additional percentage. They are attractive to some investors due to their limited risk, especially if the intention of an investor is to safeguard part of its portfolio. For example, many foreign governments own large chunks of US government's bonds, or treasury bonds, benefiting from its interest income and the strength of the US dollar.

Proponents of establishing a bond may argue that this tool is required to raise large-scale resources for businesses, or governments. There is a need, within the Muslim societies, to develop some ways to raise those funds without breaking some basic rules. At the same time, one may not ignore the fact that the conventional means of government level borrowing has resulted in mountains of debt for future generations. For example, the following is the comparison of national debt of a few countries, in terms of percentage of GDP. The USA's debt is more than 128% of what it produced every year:

	Percentage of GDP
USA	128%
UK	85%
Pakistan	87%
Saudi Arabia	31%
Singapore	132%
China	66%
Canada	116%
Germany	73%
UAE	37%
Egypt	92%
Russia	19%

To understand the impact of national debt, imagine a person living in Massachusetts and earning $50,000 a year (before taxes), and imagine that he owed $64,000 to someone else. To this amount, an additional interest amount is added every year making it an ever-expanding figure. Now, imagine how difficult it may be for the borrower to save after paying all the taxes and expenses, especially if he or she was already in the habit of spending more than what is affordable. Motivated by greed or influenced by the system in place, if pressed by the lender, the borrower may agree to pay back a small amount every month, which may just cover the interest charged on the loan. It may take at least a lifetime or a generation to pay the debt off, but even that if the borrower cared. Otherwise, this type of national loan is seldom written off and get transferred to the next generations, a financial injustice of colossal nature. The underlying fundamental problem here is not the interest or the *Riba,* it is the ill-conceived decision to borrow an amount that one cannot afford, a violation of one of the basic Islamic rules of finance.

Fact of the matter is that just like individuals, businesses and governments need to borrow. If an individual can borrow money to pay for a medical school, there is little doubt that the debt will not be paid off, or it may not be beneficial to the borrower. A country borrowing to build infrastructures like dams or airports may not be able to achieve these goals without it. The real issue is to make borrowing, at individual or at a government level, fair and just for both parties, the lender, and the borrower, as a financial injustice or deceit is ultimately what *Riba* is all about.

One option that has been used to raise large-scale money for a business or a government, for a defined project, is sharing ownership in the project instead of merely borrowing with interest. This concept is not much different from stock offering. There can be variety of ways to share part of the ownership with its profit or loss. In Islamic financial terminology this arrangement is called a *"sukuk."* In legal terminology, this is equivalent to the same concept of a promissory note, as for a bond. Despite its existence, *sukuks* have not attracted many large-scale institutional investors, like bonds did, partly due to the lack of practical examples for its large-scale use.

The Mutual Funds

The mutual funds are collection of multiple stocks, and/ or bonds taken together. As a composite, each mutual fund becomes its own entity and traded in that manner. Its allowance in Islam will depend upon its constituents.

Ideally, it shall be free of any stocks or bonds not allowed in Islam, e.g., stocks of businesses primarily dealing with *Riba*, or in an area of business otherwise not allowed, such as manufacturing or sale of non-medicinal intoxicants like most alcoholic beverages. In principle, there is no prohibition about the basic concept of a mutual fund.

The Hedge Funds

On one hand, a hedge fund seems to be any other financial advising and investment enterprise, but it is conceptually very different. At its core, it is about very rich people, or entities (like the retirement funds), contributing a lot of money to create a fund, with a hope and promise to make way more money, higher than many other ways of investing. One should know that in financial ventures, whenever the promise of reward is too high, the corresponding risk is also in that vicinity, if not more. Just like one should be careful while gambling, investing in hedge funds is recommended only for someone who can bear the loss of a large amount of money. In fact, it is not even an option for most investors. While investing, the hedge fund manager is not restricted, as a bank may be due to regulations in place, and can employ any possible investment strategy, including purchase of real estate, commodities, securities, venture capitalism, or any other financial option.

As a concept and with full truthful disclosures, hedge funds may not have an issue with Islamic financial principles, but in usual practice their managers frequently employ strategies that violate those principles. These strategies include large scale borrowing with excessive risk (or *gharar*), security short-selling, speculations, or derivative trading, all that with an idea to make money in both bearish and bullish market. The only idea is to make money, not necessarily establishing or sustaining businesses. Each hedge fund has some defined investment strategies, which an investor can explore before investing. The investment company charges a fee, usually 2%, on every dollar invested, but also receives significant portion of the profit made. Almost 50% of hedge funds fail due to one reason or the other, and a lot many under-perform. Looking at this concept in a holistic sense, there are some potential benefits to investors in it, but the risk is higher than the reward and multiple objectionable financial tools are employed, which, in totality, make the conventional hedge funds Islamically unacceptable.

What About Cryptocurrency, like the Bitcoins?

In nutshell, all Cryptocurrency is currency, carrying some value based upon multiple factors, and by itself and without any reference point, worthless. This is not much different from a dollar note, a piece of paper, which without its connotation carries not much value either. The value of a currency notes or a digital coin is based upon its origin, and its promise. Gone are the days when currency was made up of gold or silver, or the notes in circulation were backed and based upon the gold reserve a country might have to maintain. World economy now is large, global, and getting increasingly intertwined. One cannot expect to use gold and silver for sale and purchase, and in near future in paper notes either. Large part of global currency transactions is already done digitally, without any real cash changing hands. The Bitcoin is not any different in this manner.

The main difference between a dollar bill and Cryptocurrency is their backing: A currency note of

Chapter 15 – Islamic Finance in Real Life, or its Practical Implications

any country is backed by its government, while the Cryptocurrency, at least so far, has no such backing. It is a system based upon trust on a global scale, the trust upon the technology, and the market conditions. The technology maintains its strength, constantly evolving to outmaneuver any deceit or hacking. The market conditions provide its value and its fluctuations, never fully predictable. If its operation is achieved in a manner to proscribe illegal activities, it may work out well and provide an excellent global alternative to the limited and territorial national currencies. On the other hand, if not, societies may abstain from mainstreaming it, and it may just stay under the radar, like many other non-sanctioned concepts. As a concept, there is no Islamic reason to outlaw Cryptocurrency, especially if it is beneficial to the people and commerce.

Retirement Accounts, like 401k

While an average person in the USA retires in his or her mid to late 60s, the average lifespan is about 10-15 years longer, little more for woman than men. The Social Security payment, an option for most workingmen and women, does not pay enough to support comparable living after retirement. There is no universal government funded retirement plan or pension plan either. While working, people save their own money in retirement accounts, for their use later in life. This concept is consistent with Islamic teachings of dignity of hard work, responsibility, and economic prudence. Every working person, in whatever society or a field of work, must save some money for himself or herself, and their spouses. In many places, lack of this resource is a major contributing factor for family feuds, and old-age distress and abuse.

A concept not uncommon in religious circles that one should leave this issue or the issue of old-age retirement to Allah SWT alone, without any effort by an individual, is misunderstanding of the principle and spirit of Islam. As per a famous rule, in allegorical terms, one must tie the camel first before relying on Allah SWT.

Government's role in this area is to formulate appropriate rules and regulations to prevent fraud and abuse, and to promote this practice. A retirement plan is automatically available and operated for people employed in most large businesses or the governmental agencies. The problem is for the self-employed people, many in immigrant communities, not fully understanding its logic and wisdom. In most cases now, employees or individuals have the option to avoid investing in areas they may not agree with. While Muslims may have differences with certain business practices, many other people had their own reasons of not investing in certain sectors. Many retirement plan companies nowadays offer options to cater to these needs. In addition, there also are some fully "*Sharia*-compliant" capital investment companies in the USA.

It may also be worth discussing whether it is a government's responsibility, Islamic or otherwise, to provide care for retirees. For practical reasons, it can only be possible if the government has enough resources or it levied appropriate taxes, directly or indirectly, to bear the cost. This model exists in many European or otherwise rich countries. The model in the USA is different: the governments, through taxation, care for the neediest or the disabled. For most others, a private retirement account is the more dignified option as described above. Societies trying to build a retirement system may have to model an arrangement of their own, learning lessons from these examples. Sometimes, in many poor Muslim societies, there is a push to adapt a fully government funded welfare system, which can easily become a vehicle for economic and intellectual stagnation, even if the society is rich. In many other societies, their governments provide an unjust, exuberant, and lavish retirement system for the government employees, funded by the taxes paid by the larger society around them, in comparison to what is available to most of their citizens.

What About Insurance?

Archeological research has revealed that the concept of insurance against an accident or loss due to an "act of God," or a crime is an ancient economic concept, at least as old as 1750 BC. Evidence of detailed legal codes has been found in the so-called Hammurabi documentation of the Babylonian empire. Similar documents have also been found in the ruins of ancient Egyptian empire. Pre-Islamic Arabian society was quite active in trading across their borders to distant lands, including areas that were part of the Persian and Roman empires. Early Muslims travelled to distant lands through sea routes, trading with even farther away places. As one reviewed details of legal economic codes, such as in Hammurabi document, it seemed highly unlikely that pre-Islamic Arabs or early Muslim traders were unaware of this concept. While there are multiple references in the Quran and the *Hadith* about the *Riba*, there is no specific mention of insurance.

Logically speaking, early Muslims either knew the concept of insurance in trading, or they did not. If we consider that it was known, and knowing the fact that there is no direct mention of its prohibition in the Quran or the *Hadith*, one may not declare it illegal. If, on the other hand, it was not known, it will come under the category of a new concept about which no direct prohibition exists in the Quran or the *Hadith*, again making it not illegal. This is especially the case due to its multiple benefits to individuals and the society. Now let's look at some specific issues that people may have with the insurance business:

a. Collective Responsibility: The lynchpin of the insurance business is managing and minimizing risk by indemnifying it and spreading it out to a large group of people. In every society in the world, accidents, crimes, and death are part of life. A few people may be able to handle the financial repercussions after such an event, but for many others, the situation can easily become devastating. Let's look at the example of auto insurance. One may easily compare a society with proper auto insurance where the impact of an accident on the people involved in the accident is tremendously different. In one system with proper insurance (e.g., the USA), the automobile is repaired, injuries are treated, and life for all parties moves on. While, in a system without such insurance (e.g., Pakistan), most of the treatment, repair and compensation is not guaranteed. People are routinely left with personal injuries without treatment, damages to their automobiles, and the property un-repaired. In most cases, matters are settled in an unjust, discriminatory, and frequently in a cruel manner. One may say that the Pakistani society has refused to take proper actions and fulfill their collective responsibility.

Chapter 15 – Islamic Finance in Real Life, or its Practical Implications

The compensatory payment for an incident is made by the funds collected from the larger uninvolved population, with their fully informed consent and agreement, not through duress or taxation. There is no specific injunction against this concept in the Quran or the *Hadith*. On the contrary, pre-Islamic Arabs and early Muslim tribes used a similar concept to pay large amounts of resources or money, to compensate a deceased's family (the *Qisas*), if their tribe member(s) was involved in a killing. This practice not only diluted the risk of financial loss, but also provided a reliable system of compensation, and promoted collective responsibility: a win-win situation for both an individual and the society.

b. The *Riba*: Some people may take the position that an additional amount given to an individual, in case of a damage or an accident, more than the premium amount, is *Riba* and not allowed. As elaborated in a previous chapter in detail, and in the example above, not every additional amount is *Riba*.

It was important to mention that there is a difference between insurance against a damage or disaster, and a bet. Just like damages and disasters, win or a loss are also parts of daily life. While an arrangement of a system of insurance against damages from accident or disasters can be justified (using the cost-benefit analysis), similar arrangement against a loss in a game is a bet or gambling, something clearly outlawed by the Quran. The key is the matter of intention, and its benefit to the society. Every such situation requires a similar cost-benefit analysis before reaching the right conclusion.

What About Commodity Trading?

A commodity can be an agricultural product, a mineral, or a similar item such as oil & gas. Islam allows purchasing commodities in advance, with a clear, well-defined written agreement. We are prohibited from re-selling it without first taking its full custody and inspection, especially for agricultural products. Speculative trading is not allowed, as it implies ownership of something one may not afford and may not be able to pay its price off, and sale of something one does not own or have. As much as possible, the middleman concept is discouraged, and trading between a producer and consumers is promoted. In the present-day world of global industrialization, avoiding middle channel, like a wholesaler, is not a practical option. It is interesting to note though, that modern grocery stores, or departmental stores like Walmart or Amazon, despite being in the middle, in a way facilitate producer-to-customer access. More realistic examples of such kind in USA are the Flea markets or the Farmer's markets.

While making a contract to purchase a commodity on a future date, or within a certain duration, is allowed in Islam, it is against re-selling something without taking its possession. This means that buying and selling commodities, or commodity stocks, with no intention of owning or taking its possession is not allowed. This is for benefit of both the buyer and the seller. While making a contract, as much as possible, potential risk of avoidable harm to either trading party (the *dharar*), or any type of avoidable uncertainty (or the *gharar*), must be avoided.

Chapter 15 – Islamic Finance in Real Life, or its Practical Implications

Future and Options

To understand concepts like the "futures" or the "options," at least for some readers, it may be useful to review some basic financial concepts. In a marketplace, there are multiple ways to trade and make money. For the sake of simplicity and explanation, I divide them as follows:

A: Direct Sale: This is when a producer of a product (e.g., a farmer or a manufacturer) directly sells the product to the end-user. The product in this example may be a practically or physically useable item, or even a service. In this arrangement, the producer is the only party making a profit. Islam promotes this type of trading.

B: Indirect Sale: In this arrangement, a farmer or a producer may sell their products to an intermediary channel, before they reach the users. Depending upon a particular location or a product, there may be more than one intermediary channel, and many parties earning a profit. In situations where it may result in significant loss to a producer, and direct sale is possible and practical, Islam discourages intermediary channels.

C: Being a Producer: Ownership may be full or partial, e.g., through company stocks. As every stockholder carries a proportional ownership with associated benefits and risks, there is no Islamic prohibition about it. When investing in an Islamic manner, thorough research about the company is recommended, so that a calculated intelligent decision is made. Wasting and carelessness about the resources is un-Islamic.

D: Indirect Investing: This is where it starts to get tricky. For example, investing in mutual funds, at its core, is still like investing in stocks with similar risks and benefits. The usual purpose of investing in mutual funds is diversification, longer-term benefit, and, depending on the funds picked for investment, there may still be no clear violation of any Islamic rule.

E: Speculations: If one studies the above-described rules of Islamic finance, it is not difficult to figure out that their basic purpose is to minimize harm to either trading party, or to remove uncertainties as much as possible. Speculative trading carries disproportionate risks, while promising an unrealistic reward. The purpose of speculative trading is not about producing any product or providing any service, it is purely a financial gameplay. Like any professional sport, people who play it very well, do make out big, at least in the short-term, but almost everyone else loses every penny. The concepts around speculative trading are inherently complex and deceiving. Examples of speculative trading included trading in Futures, Margins, or Derivatives. Even if done using a valid company and its stock, this type of trading may easily violate multiple basic Islamic rules of finance and may not be permitted.

Let's study them individually:

a. **Futures:** In a nutshell, in financial terms, a future is a contract to buy or sell a product at a fixed predetermined price at a certain date, despite whatever the price of that product may be at that time. This arrangement carries a significant risk of damage to the buyer or the seller, if the price of the product differ considerably, while adding a preventable uncertainty. In general, this type of trading does not provide any significant benefit to the society either. Understanding all that, Islamic rules do not permit this type of arrangement. To be fair to both parties, one may decide to buy the same product at a certain date at the market-price of the day. This arrangement may still carry an uncertainty about the price of the product, but that is fair to both parties, and not completely preventable.

This rule is valid for products that are already available to trade. For products that require time, sometimes months to years to produce, it is flexible. For example, it is allowed to decide with a farmer to buy his crop within a certain future timeframe in years, at a pre-determined price. Same analogy can be applied while making a contract with a manufacturer, extractor of oil & gas, or a builder. Reasons for its justification include benefit to both parties, and overall, to the society.

b. **Options:** While trading in stocks or mutual funds is about trading a product, albeit in smaller fractions, the investor hoped for and benefits if a company or the companies do well. Trading in options is a seemingly similar but an altogether different concept. It is not about investing in a business or a company, it is rather a monetary gameplay based upon ups and downs of a company's stock, or the stock market. Like most sports, there is a winner and a loser, a zero-sum game, with no real intention of establishing, sustaining, or fostering a business. Between the investor and the option trader, one party's loss is other party's win. In essence, trading in options is a bet on a company's gain or loss, and not an investment in its stock. Depending how the bet is placed, the investor may be betting on the company's gain or the loss. In fact, an astute investor may bet on both options of a gain or a loss, in a way, losing only if there is not much change in the company's value. To most option investors, who are technically amateurs, it seems an attractive opportunity to make a lot of money. But most never reach that goal, unaware that the odds, like gambling, are mostly designed to favor the option trader. I compare option trading to betting in horse or dog racing, or cock fighting (in some cultures), or any similar activity. One may call it intelligent gambling, but it is still a gamble. Neither party has any interest in wellbeing of the company (or the horse, the cock, or the dog), if they can place their bets and make their fortunes.

As for as the concept of a hedge against a loss, a commonly stated reason for this practice, including even by some Islamic analysts to justify its permissibility, it is akin to betting on multiple horses or dogs in a race, or both cocks in a fight. As an analogy, it is also like stating that to safeguard portfolio of investment in meat business, a Muslim is allowed to invest in pork bellies. I am not sure how that can be permissible. Finally, the idea of "necessity" to justify its legality seems far-fetched, which is an allowance in Islamic law but invoked in critical situations.

c: **Shorting stocks:** There are numerous problems with this type of trading. Like option trading, basic impetus for shorting stocks is to make unrealistic amount of money while not even having proper amount of cash in hand to invest. It involves borrowing money with excessive amount of mark-up by the lender, the classic *Riba*, in fact the kind of *Riba* specifically prohibited by the Quran. The arrangements for shorting involved excessive unreasonable risk, or *gharar*, which may easily lead to financial ruins. The investor has no interest in the company's wellbeing; in fact, they are betting against its success. This concept is contrary to numerous fundamental Islamic rules and cannot be permissible.

d: Margin trading: Like shorting stocks, margin trading means making an investment with money one does not have. It is trading with borrowed money with high interest rate or *Riba*. People are attracted to it to bet on large number of stocks, which for them may lose, or gain in value. In real life though, one can never completely predict the direction a stock may take, up or down, and when it goes in the wrong direction, they lose not only the money they contribute but also much more, going into formidable financial debt or ruins. Because of significant *dharar* and *gharar*, it cannot be permissible in Islam.

e: Gambling: Gambling is a routine part of business in most countries, unfortunately including Islamic countries. Let's look at the concept of gambling first: the dictionary definition of gambling is, a. game of chance for money, a bet, b. taking risky actions in the hope of a desired result. There are numerous ways and opportunities to gamble in the USA, from a grocery store payment console to a variety of ways in neighborhoods, and then elaborate and extravagant casinos. It is both ubiquitous and insidious, and easily addictive. Gambling machine operation is based upon well-established and sophisticated mathematical algorithms, which make sure that the "player", or rather the victim, is lured with flashes and glitters, but more importantly by some incremental wins. Unfortunately, for most gamblers, the fun and enjoyment of smaller wins follows an inevitable much bigger loss. There is no monetary benefit to anyone other than the gambling company, or rarely an occasional winner, and that if only he or she walks away with it. Islam specifically forbids this practice.

A variant of this practice is lottery business. Here the situation gets somewhat murky. In the USA, the state lottery system is designed primarily to raise funds for public projects, like roads, bridges, and schools. It is a significant source of income for most states and for many states the income from the lottery is more than the state tax collection. Conceptually speaking and in Islamic terms, this type of lottery can be compared to alcohol, which may have some benefits for humans, but it has more harm than benefit. Even in the USA, it is illegal some states, due to religious reasons.

f: The Swaps: In financial terms, a swap contract is somewhat unregulated business contracting where parties try to minimize the financial risk arising from certain factors, like the fluctuations in the foreign currency exchange rates, failure or default of a bond issuing company, fluctuations of interest rates on loans, or fluctuations in the price of commodities. There are many variations based upon a particular situation or a need. At the end, it is meant to be an insurance against a potential loss, while it may also be an intelligent bet by a shrewd investor. Some contracts may

Chapter 15 – Islamic Finance in Real Life, or its Practical Implications

very well be useful and result in win-win for both parties. But some, may carry excessive amount of risk, almost like gambling. Every situation requires a review, as the former may be *halal*, but the latter may not be.

The Day-trading

Unlike a long-term investor, a day-trader buys and sells products, in this case commodities and stocks, on same day, or in a short time, sometimes within minutes to hours. Despite its tremendous risks, technically speaking and as per Islamic rules, it is not impermissible. For understanding, let's look at two ancient trading practices: many people were involved in long-term investments and trading, e.g., the Prophet's first wife, may Allah SWT be pleased with her. She managed trading caravans taking material from Arabia to distant places, which required significant investment, skill, commitment, and patience. This can be compared to any present-day long-term investment. But there also were people who took one Dinar, went to the marketplace, bought a product, sold it with a profit, bought another product with the proceeds, and sold it again making another profit, all within a short amount of time. This is a reasonably good comparison to what we now call day-trading.

While day-trading may be allowed in Islam, it still carries significant risk, which we are advised to avoid. While dealing with risky financial situations, one is always in danger of deviating further and indulging in speculations and gambling. Here, I am reminded of a famous *hadith* of the Prophet SAW, which (paraphrasing) stated that there are acts that are clearly *haram* (not allowed) or *halal* (allowed), but then there also are acts with some uncertainties, in a way a slippery slope. Using this notion, for most people, the day-trading done by individual investors, which is mostly done without proper training or research about the companies, is seldom profitable and best avoided.

The Professions

It may be useful to provide a few comments about the types of profession one may use to earn money or resources. Whatever profession one may pick up, one must follow the fundamental Islamic principles of fairness or justice, truthfulness, and avoidance of *gharar* and *dharar*. A profession or an activity harmful to others: humans, life-forms, or the nature, in any shape or form, is against the spirit of Islam. In addition, the Quran and the *Hadith* specifically prohibit some professional activities, which may directly or indirectly involve dealing with something *haram*, such as, gambling, prostitution, or harmful drugs. While begging is strongly discouraged, value of work, or relying on earned money, is equally well emphasized in the *Hadith*.

A common struggle within the immigrant community relying on relatively accessible and inexpensive means to earn their living, such as the business of local convenient stores, frequently involve dealing with items not allowed in Islam, e.g., the pork meat, gambling, or the alcoholic beverages. Interesting aspect of this issue is that people usually are reliant to deal with pork, but not as much with alcohol, and lesser so with gambling. As per Islamic rules, all these activities are equally prohibited.

Even more bizarre, though rare, is the notion that one may lie or cheat a non-Muslim or in a non-Muslim society (somewhat like some Jewish understanding that one may charge

Chapter 15 – Islamic Finance in Real Life, or its Practical Implications

Riba to a non-Jewish person). People need a reminder that the Quran and the *Hadith* do not allow or justify any such negative activity, or make such moral exception, irrespective of the situation or the people involved. There is a concept of "necessity" in *Sharia*, like the allowance of eating pork meat, if the alternate option is starvation to death. But that is not a justifiable option even if it is the only available meat, and a vegetarian option is available. This kind of issues are better understood if one appreciates the concept of internal consistency described in a previous chapter. Allowance based upon necessity is only an option if the necessity is critical, and the alternate option carry a significantly destructive or a fatal course. In analogical terms, the basis of this concept is derived from the Quran, from an *ayah* that discuss the type of meat not allowed to eat:

The Quran, Al-Maidah, *ayah* 3 (Al-Qruan 5:3):

> "Forbidden to you (for food) are: dead meat, blood, the flesh of swine, and that on which hath been invoked the name of other than Allah; that which hath been killed by strangling, or by a violent blow, or by a headlong fall, or by being gored to death; that which hath been (partly) eaten by a wild animal; unless ye are able to slaughter it (in due form); that which is sacrificed on stone (altars); (forbidden) also is the division (of meat) by raffling with arrows, that is impiety. This day have those who reject Faith given up all hope of our religion: yet fear them not but fear Me. This day have I perfected your religion for you, completed my favour upon you, and have chosen for you Islam as your religion. **But if any is forced by hunger, with no inclination to transgression, Allah is indeed Oft-Forgiving, Most Merciful.**" Ali.

"Forbidden to you (for food) are: *Al-Maytatah* (the dead animals – cattle-beast not slaughtered), blood, the flesh of swine, and the meat of that which has been slaughtered as a sacrifice for others than Allah, or has been slaughtered for idols, etc., or on which Allah's Name has not been mentioned while slaughtering, and that which has been killed by strangling, or by a violent blow, or by a headlong fall, or by the goring of horns – and that which has been (partly) eaten by a wild animal – unless you are able to slaughter it (before its death) – and that which is sacrificed (slaughtered) on *An-Nusub* (stone altars). (Forbidden) also is to use arrows seeking luck or decision, (all) that is *Fisqun* (disobedience of Allah and sin). This day, those who disbelieved have given up all hope of your religion, so fear them not, but fear Me. This day, I have perfected your religion for you, completed My Favour upon you, and have chosen for you Islam as your religion. **But as for him who is forced by severe hunger, with no inclination to sin (such can eat these above-mentioned meats), then surely, Allah is Oft-Forgiving, Most Merciful.**"Al-Hilali & Khan.

What religiously is allowed and not allowed, even in terms of a professional activity, is a matter (religiously speaking) between a person and Allah SWT. There is no way for anyone to know any other person's full situation, or the intention. Someone may ask for an advice or an opinion in this matter, and one may provide an educated answer, i.e., advice based upon the Quran and the *Hadith*, but may not and shall not force anyone towards a particular course. It is up to an individual to

Chapter 15 – Islamic Finance in Real Life, or its Practical Implications

understand that one day he or she shall stand in front of Allah SWT and defend whatever course is chosen. There definitely is no reason to argue with someone who does not even believe in that inevitable outcome.

The International Monetary Fund (IMF)

Finance is not just a local concept, especially in the increasingly closer global world. Despite their physical boundaries, and separate financial systems, countries are still interdependent. So much so that even a relatively poor country's problems may significantly impact the international monetary situation. If a country's economic system collapses, it may impact its creditors or the international investors. Depending upon the size of a country, or its economy, the impact may be devastating resulting ultimately in devaluation of other countries' currencies. To safeguard against this type of problem, an international institution, the IMF, was created in 1944. Its main purpose was to prop up a troubled economy and to avoid its collapse, which ultimately helps to avoid international recession, a win-win situation for the troubled country and the world.

IMF is funded by a relatively just system. Every member country contributes a sum, its quota, which is based upon the size of its economy and other factors. This pooled money is used to fund loans generated by the IMF. IMF loans carry an interest or a charge, which generally is very small; for today it is 1.05%, but for poor countries, it may be zero percent, the so-called *qard e hasanah*. So, IMF technically is an international charity for the countries, not a business, and its mission is to help countries come out of financial crises. While giving the money, it coaxes and sometimes requires the borrowing country to adapt certain financial reforms. Major elements of these reforms include controlling corruption, adjusting lucrative government benefit plans, controlling other subsidies, closing, or adjusting businesses or ventures that may be losing money, investing in infrastructure that may help everyone, and improving taxation system. Many elements of these reforms frequently conflict with the interests of the ruling class of an affected country. Despite that, countries usually agree to make changes and pay back the loan. Default rate is very low, because if the payments are not made, no one else in the world is willing to help, and the country may get economically outcasted, a fate no one wants. Most countries of the world are its members, and it is ruled not by any country, but rather by a board of governors.

Technically, there is no Islamic conflict with the concept and mission of IMF. Of note, currently, two of the largest beneficiary countries from IMF are Egypt and Pakistan.

The World Bank

While the main mission of IMF is to support a country's economy by supporting its currency or the foreign currency reserves, the World Bank is an international bank with a similar mission but a different mode of action. It was also established in 1940s by rich countries. Like the IMF, most countries of the world have directly or indirectly benefited from its services. Its main mission is to fight extreme poverty, by supporting (not fully funding) economic projects in poor countries. Like a bank, most loans are not free, though the interest rates are significantly lower than conventional commercial banks. Sometimes, for very poor countries, the loans are interest free. It funds projects that may help bring a country's population out of poverty, like a dam for irrigation

Chapter 15 – Islamic Finance in Real Life, or its Practical Implications

or an educational grant for primary education. The funding is a partnership between the country and the bank, with the country always having a stake in any venture. Its main source of funding includes the donation from rich countries, investments, assets, and return on the loans made.

While talking about IMF and the World Bank, it may be useful to mention that there is an element of controversy about their influence or real intentions, or the intentions of the people or the countries funding them. This subject is beyond the scope of this book, though I say that one may find multiple countries and societies who benefited from these institutions and rebuilt their economies, while many others could not replicate it despite multiple interventions. At the end of the day, the most important factors for economic growth and success, for individuals or countries, are not much different. Freedom of action, an intention and the will to work, equality and respect for the rule of law, and most importantly a will to defend all of that at any cost. Individuals and countries may get financially devastated mostly due to their own wrong choices, decisions, and policies. As outlined below, even Allah SWT's help, and blessing is not without a condition:

The Quran, Al-Rad, *ayah* 11 (Al-Quran 13:11):

"… Verily never will Allah change the condition of a people until they change it themselves (with their own souls)…" Ali.

"… Verily! Allah will not change the (good) condition of a people as long as they do not change their state (of goodness) themselves (by committing sins and by being ungrateful and disobedient to Allah)…" Al-Hilali & Khan.

The Interest Rates

Someone may rightly ask, why am I even discussing the interest rate, if it is the forbidden *Riba*? The answer to that question is provided in detail above, but also that even the so-called Islamic financing institutions ultimately use a figure, a bench-mark rate, to calculate and formulate the "mark-up" in an "Islamic" financial contract, like an Islamic mortgage. It may be helpful to know the ultimate origin of this number.

Most loans in the world are made by banks, not by individuals, and almost all are not free, both in Islamic and non-Islamic countries. As most banks are not working in an Islamic manner or following one of the "Dodd-Frank" rules by which they may not lend more than they can afford to lose and to keep their lending business going, they routinely borrow from each other. For some odd reason, this borrowing happens when the banks are closed, or at night, and it is called inter-bank borrowing. The rate a lending bank charged the other bank is called the inter-bank borrowing rate. This is an important number, as it is reflective of the market conditions at the time of borrowing, not just an arbitrary number.

The most famous inter-bank borrowing rate is called the LIBOR, the London Interbank Offered Rate, which is calculated daily based upon a complex process that involve most major banks and their input. Every other country in the world, and for that matter, every other financial or lending institution, relies on this number. If LIBOR goes up, the interest rates move up too, and vice versa. In a way, this is a government-controlled system to maintain a fair marketplace and to avoid unjust surcharges. This contrasted with the old-fashioned arbitrary lending system where the lender could have come up or enforce any amount of surcharge on a loan. Recently, there has been a lot of criticism against the LIBOR, and a new and more sophisticated similar system may start operating in future, the so-called Secured Overnight Financing Rate (SOFR). As I stated above, making the system of borrowing and lending fair and just is an ongoing process.

As far as the Islamic lending institutions are concerned, ultimately, they also rely on and use the same number, the LIBOR now, and will likely use the SOFR in near future, to calculate the "mark-up" on the loans they generate.

After the LIBOR, the second most important factor or control on the interest rate is a country's central bank, which lowers or elevates it to achieve a government's policy goals, such as maintaining value of its currency, or economic stability, which benefits everyone in the society.

Economic Boycott

Human being is a socio-political entity with complexities of value systems based upon multiple factors including the family, religion, ethnicity, ethics, nationality, and the choice of political affiliations. Nations, even large and rich nations, are not any different. They forge relationships with other countries primarily for, besides many others, business interests. Despite ideological differences, and at times, overt conflicts, every country strives to keep good relations with others to continue benefiting from its economic benefit, a well-known and well-understood mutual dependance. But sometimes, this element of reliance is used, or abused, to settle or fight a political conflict. For whatever reasons, it is quite common for one country to not or limit trade with another, but at times, a whole swath of countries working together may decide to boycott a country or countries for political reasons. Whether it is fair or just, or unjust, is a different matter and unique to every situation, but in principle, this practice is allowable in Islam. Any country, especially a suppressed society, is allowed to not cooperate, resist, or reject any economic cooperation, especially if it is detrimental to their interests. At the same time, an unjust boycott (or breaking proper relations) by or against a person, a family, or a society is un-Islamic, as it may result in unjustifiable suffering.

Offshore Companies and Offshore Banking

There can be a genuine or an honest reason to incorporate a business in a place away from home, or some other place one is not directly related to, but in many cases this option is used by rich to get richer using illegal means (e.g., by not paying proper taxes), or the criminals to hide income from an illegal business. The localities offering these services, and their customers, are either abusing some loopholes in the system, i.e., business and banking regulations, or violating them. If the basic intent of this activity is to cheat the system, which in a lot of cases is the problem, it violates multiple Islamic rules and is not allowed.

Smuggling and Money Laundering

Even discussing these topics here seems odd, but some people take these activities as their livelihood. They are illegal activities with no Islamic basis. These activities require lying, deceiving, cheating, many other associated criminal activities, and breaking multiple local or international laws. Breaking the established laws of a state or a country one is a resident of or visiting does not have any Islamic basis. The excuse that, "there was no other or profitable way to make money" – an argument also used by people involved in the illicit drug trade – does not have any Islamic basis. Using the cost-benefit analysis rule in this type of situations is at best a perversion.

A War or Fighting

Equally absurd is the concept of war and fighting in the present discussion but there is a reason. Some countries have used this option to wage illegal or unjust wars. During the 16th and 17th century, the East India Company of the United Kingdom working in the Indian subcontinent was much more than a business, it worked as "hired guns," and fought with locals by using every ethical or unethical means at their disposal. In recent past, the USA government hired private contractors for similar military missions, and some of their techniques were not much different either. There are many other countries in the world utilizing "proxy" fighters, but technically that is considered an illegal activity. While these companies, involved or fighting on behalf of the USA, were legal enterprises paying taxes. One of the main justifications for utilizing them, a reason usually not made clear to the public, is to accomplish goals through illegal means, means that violate the established international rules of war. In case their illegal actions are ever discovered, the military and the politicians use the concept of plausible deniability and remain indifferent.

In Islam, a war or a fight is never a business. It is not done for business either, unless someone is trying to illegally restrict this activity. Only the state is allowed to declare and conduct a war, not individuals or groups. All participants are required to follow strict code of conduct. For Muslims, the rules of a conflict or a war are defined by the Quran and the Prophet SAW, by his words and actions, as he took part in multiple battles. On international level, modern rules of war were established during the 19th and the 20th centuries. For a Muslim to take part in a war, on behalf of the state, is a very sacred duty and not done for material reasons. It is done for Allah SWT and its reward is expected from Him alone. There is monetary benefit of military service, as for many it is more of a profession than a mission, but anyone involved in it just for material reasons, or as a business, is acting against Islamic ethics and rules.

Chapter 16

Islamic Economy & Corporate Governance

Humans are tribal being and most of us are either associated with or belong to a group. The group we belong to may be as small as our own family or quite large, like a country or even beyond. The reasons for belonging or associating with a group may not be a matter of choice, but many times it is. While belonging to our family or a country is mostly not in our control, many other associations we start and cultivate are entirely volitional. These associations and grouping, volitional or not, necessitate from us some level of teamwork. Teamwork or working as a group requires establishing some fundamental guiding principles, rules, and ways of operation. This is true at every level and for every organization, from a small family to a whole citizenry of a country. Success and long-term outlook of each group or its group-effort depends upon its foundational principles, its modus operandi, and their proper application.

For this chapter, the group I am concentrating upon is the one organized for a business. This discussion may also be applicable to not-for-profit entities, or a solo or a family enterprise. Every corporation, even between two partners or of any size, is formulated for a specific purpose. For most corporations in the world, their main purpose or the mission is to make more money.

Making money is important for an individual, a group, or a country, as their physical and social wellbeing and survival depends upon it. Countries and civilizations, especially on the larger and longer scale, fail and falter more often due to economic reasons than a military defeat. This has been the story of the British empire, and the Soviet Union. Even for a small country, like Pakistan, its long-term survival is linked less to its military power and more to its economic progress, as the former can only survive if the latter thrives. Unfortunately, many countries or at least their military leadership read this lesson other way around, resulting in perpetual failures. This is an interesting socio-economic subject but not the topic of this writing. Here, I am bringing attention to the subject of business or corporate failure in some societies, like Pakistan. I discuss these weaknesses, which are embedded in their socio-legal culture, restricting their ability to succeed and compete.

The success of a group or a society is directly proportional to how effectively it can work as a group. This applies to all aspects of the society, especially to its business enterprise. As the success of business enterprise is directly linked to overall wellbeing of a society, any improvement in this area is beneficial to all its segments. But entrepreneurship is a difficult task and not everyone's cup of tea. Most feel comfortable finding a "job," or a service job, instead of creating businesses or means of employment for other people. Not only that, the leadership of a country can also be disillusioned and short-sighted and keeps on replicating employment opportunities from the same or pre-existing economic pie, breaking it into smaller and smaller pieces, instead of taking steps to increase the size of the pie. This type of policies and their direct and indirect impact, promoted by disillusioned and corrupt politicians, may bring the society to its ruins. Political parties and their elites fail these societies, both at ideological and operational levels, another fascinating topic to discuss, but not the topic of this discussion.

My parent's families were forced immigrants in Pakistan from the Indian side of the Punjab in 1947. Many elders of the family were killed, including my grandfather. Most of the family resources were either confiscated or lost. Many family members survived the ordeal, but they were left with meagre resources and lack of any real direction. Looking back, in economic terms, I see that most of my family members struggled while some succeeded, and a few have done quite well. Some have been able to build medium sized manufacturing businesses from scratch, providing employment for hundreds of families, a praiseworthy achievement in any society. In the USA, similar businesses, within the timeframe they succeeded and the extent of business opportunities they enjoyed, could easily have morphed themselves into much larger enterprises, or at least be bought up by a larger corporation. But I expect none of that to happen to my family's enterprises. I expect these businesses to be closed as soon as the generation that started them passes away. Such entrepreneurial demise is not so unique, it is a common unfortunate occurrence in a society like

Pakistan. The root cause of this unfortunate fate is not just their "fate" or even their competition, it has a lot to do with poor corporate governance.

The issue of poor corporate governance is not just a problem of family-owned or operated businesses, many larger and even the so-called multi-national enterprises may have the same problem. In some countries, this problem may be so widespread that very few businesses compete at international level or achieve their potential goals. The price of this problem for the society can be very high, depriving it the source of wealth and means of hundreds of thousands of employment opportunities.

If we compare richer countries or economically more successful countries to the one that are struggling, one common differentiating factor is better governance, both at governmental and corporate level. This does not mean that businesses do not fail in richer or successful societies. It is just that the chances of further success and expansion for a successful smaller enterprise is much higher in societies with better corporate governance. While I discuss the issue of corporate governance, I cannot ignore the impact of governmental policies and operations as they are intertwined with each other. In the following pages, I break this subject into smaller topics to help us understand its different pieces. But first, I discuss some basic relevant economic concepts:

An Economy and its Different Types: Which one is good for me?

Some understanding of this aspect of economics is essential for everyone, because without this understanding, one can easily be taken advantage of and unfortunately this is happening everywhere all the time, especially in less developed societies like Pakistan. Without this understanding, people, including those directly involved with business and entrepreneurial activities, are misled, their interests manipulated, and their rights violated both by the governmental bureaucracies and the political elites. This phenomenon may be more obvious in autocratic societies but is equally noticeable and may be more economically damaging in societies with limited education and inadequate intellectual prowess.

Economies are of two types: a. The so-called "public" or government-owned, and b. Private-owned. In economic terminology, a public-owned economy is called a command economy, and the private-owned a free-market economy. The term command means that someone or some entity is in command or control of the economy, in this case the government, who may also assume its ownership. Example of such an economy is a communist system where the government has the total ownership, on behalf of all citizens or the public. In this case, government also has control on all resources, their allocation and utilization. The idea is to consider everyone, in fiscal terms, equal with joined ownership of assets, expect from them same amount of work, though type of work may differ, and pay them somewhat in equivalent terms. In this type of system, there is little incentive to work hard or to innovate. As human beings, in many aspects, are never equal, and never agree on equal ownership, not even in a communist system, this system of entrepreneurial governance utterly failed in the USSR and doomed that empire. In its hay day, many other societies, or their political elites, were partly or fully impressed and adapted the same model, some completely and many partially. North Korea and Cuba adapted it completely, and Pakistan did it partially.

A variant of command economy is the one owned by a monarch. Monarchy in the present world has mostly dwindled or in most cases has become only ceremonial, except in some places where it still controls large part of the country's economy, e. g., Brunei or Saudi Arabia.

The opposite of a public-owned or command economy is the private-owned or free-market economy. It means that there is no one person, or any government, owning or controlling it. Rather, the only controlling factor is the market, which is free from any governmental interference, as much as possible. In this system, in fiscal terms, people are not equal, some have more, and others have lesser ownership of resources. People are also free to work hard, which they usually do, innovate, and try to increase their ownership even further. Realistically, there is no such example of a completely private-owned or totally free-market economy. It is only a theoretical economic concept. But one can provide examples of pockets of such economies within a larger financial system. This type of economy has its own shortcomings and can easily fail too. The main reason for its failure is excessive human selfishness, which if not somewhat controlled can easily doom any financial system.

In today's world, most economies are a mixture of the above two types, public or government owned and private-owned, or command and free-market types. Because of this mix, and for sake of better practical understanding, I have divided them further in following five groups. This classification does not address many other concerns a society may value, like human rights or

Chapter 16 – Islamic Economy & Corporate Governance

the environmental issues. So that one may understand the practical impact of this classification, I provide a fiscal parameter, the per capita GDP in 2020 for countries mentioned (per capita GDP is the gross value of the economy divided by its population, which reflects how well-off citizens of these societies are). Also, in some cases, a country's economy may have significant governmental ownership, but it can still be remarkably free, i.e., mostly dictated by market forces instead of governmental interference.

World Economies

1. Restricted: Most economic activities are under governmental control with little bit of relaxations here and there. Examples are North Korea (per capita GDP about $2,000) or Cuba (per capita GDP about $10,000).

2. Controlled: These economies are controlled by the government but the restrictions on economic activities are not as much as the group above. In the examples I provide, these economies historically were more controlled and were failing when their governments decided to loosen some control and let free-market entrepreneurships thrive. The control in these economies is still so strong that it can always impact or curtail its free-market potentials. Examples are Russia (per capita GDP about $12,000), and China (per capita GDP about $12,500).

3. Less controlled: These economies are somewhat less controlled by the governments, but the government still has a significant ownership,

influence, and interfering power, due to either a monarchial system, like in Saudi Arabia (per capita GDP about $23,500), or the so-called semi-government enterprises, like in Pakistan (per capita GDP about $15,00). Most struggling economies belong to this group. Here it is important to mention that a large part of Saudi Arabian GDP is from oil and gas production and export, a factor of "Economic Goldmine", which I address later in the discussion.

4. Relatively free: At this level, there is much more freedom for any type of economic activity, but there are restrictions, some justified by the governments due to national security concerns, and others for different reasons, such as political, social, or religious. Most developed and thriving economies belong to this group. Examples are Germany (per capita GDP about $51,000) or the United States of America (per capita GDP $69,000).

5. Free: I am not sure if any country's economy is totally free from governmental ownership and interference but, in the present context, some economies are freer than most other. Examples are Singapore (per capita GDP $78,000) and Switzerland (per capita GDP $93,500).

Looking at this grouping, it is easy to find a trend, economies get larger and better for its citizens as we go down the list. Going down the list imply greater private ownership, higher level of economic freedom, and higher level of reliance on the concept of free-market or market control instead of governmental interference. At the same time, it is important to reiterate that a "free" economy is not free of sensible governmental rules and regulations. On the contrary, suitable governmental rules and regulations is the key for its growth and expansion.

An important question for a Muslim is : what kind of economic model or economy does Islam recommend ? I bring this question to the forefront due to the value many Muslim societies portray in their systems. My understanding is that the first two levels of economic models described above, the restricted and the controlled, do not have any Islamic basis. They in fact violate many basic Islamic rules of finance. In my opinion, the Islamic model of finance is the option 4, or the relatively free model. It is also not the last one as Islam restricts some types of financial activities.

In an Islamic economic system, people are free to own financial resources, i.e., the private ownership, and anyone or the state may not usurp this right without a valid justification and compensation. An Islamic state does not get involved in establishing or running enterprises, it regulates them. There are always exceptions, if they are made with full consensus of the population instead of arbitrary rulings or for the benefit of a distinct group. This must be done with appropriate guardrails to prevent corruption and cronyism. The primary responsibility of the state in this context is to provide and maintain a fair and relatively free financial environment for entrepreneurs to bloom, thrive, and bear fruit for the whole society. At the same time, the state provides appropriate controlling regulations, and a fair system of governance for any litigation, to troubleshoot, and to implement basic Islamic constraints.

Ownership vs Entrepreneurship

It is important to understand these terms as they are not synonymous. A person can be the owner of an asset (e.g., land, money, or a business), which is relatively easy to understand and figure out. Entrepreneurship on the other hand is different concept. One way to define entrepreneurship is that it is the ability to envision and manage a money-making project effectively and successfully. A successful entrepreneur is not just a good manager of an ongoing project, he or she is good in envisioning and starting a new idea or a project, or a new business. This kind of ability on a larger scale has always differentiated successful or progressive families or societies from others. While mere ownership of assets, depending upon their type and value, may make people rich or not in a need of work, it may also make those assets unavailable for further growth, a concept Islam discourages. Ownership and entrepreneurship are two different mindsets, though they are not mutually exclusive, anyone can be either of those, or both. But whatever option one picks up, it has its repercussions to that individual, his or her family, and the whole society.

Let me use an example to explain it further. Let's say a family of 4, 5 or even more people (parents with 2, 3, or more children) owns a small piece of agricultural land, an acre or two or a few acres, not uncommon in many places in Pakistan. The land, if it is cultivated in the usual manner, is not enough to sustain even a single family. The family may opt to rent it out for some yearly income, but that amount may not be enough for its primary source of income. Many times, the land is not even cultivable. This is an example of ownership and its benefits and limitations.

Using the same example in a different family where someone may come up with an idea to use this land differently, while even maintaining its ownership, to undertake a project that may significantly increase family's income. This idea can be a farming project, like a unique crop, something related to agriculture, like a quail farm, or something altogether different, like a solar farm. This type of thinking and activity is called entrepreneurship. If done right, any of these ideas has the potential to be more lucrative. In most cases though, this kind of approach is not taken resulting in missed opportunities for the family. There are variety of reasons for this not to happen and I try to comment on some of them as follows.

Family Disharmony

Few families are harmonious enough to make right decisions about their collective wellbeing, but then these are the ones who may be successful and thriving. A family comprises of a group of people, sometimes just two. The biggest problem with a group like a family is the lack of understanding of its proper functioning. A family is the smallest democratic unit, sometimes just husband and wife, though most, mistakenly, consider it autocratic. One of the reasons is that people misunderstand democracy. In democracy, both husband and wife (and the adult children) have the same say, but one of them must always lead. There is no concept of democracy without a leader, and the primary role of a leader is to provide direction. Once chosen, it is imperative to follow the leader's lead (Al-Quran 4:59). In most cases, reaching a goal requires making multiple decisions and taking several steps. In a democracy, decisions are made with consultation and agreement with each other, not coerced or forced (Al-Quran 42:38).

There can be disagreement within the group, which is beneficial instead of harmful, and not everyone may agree with a certain point of view. At the end, there must be a mechanism in place to make decisions, and this is where the role of the leader becomes important. He or she tries to bring everyone on board, or at least the majority. At the end, in a democracy, the leader also has an additional power, the power to veto a decision. This power is useful and works best if only used in exceptional or rare situations.

In a true democratic system, at least a simple majority (more than 50%) is needed to make any decision. In this manner, in a family of husband and wife, any decision made without other person's consent is not democratic and can easily lead to multiple issues within and outside the family. Another aspect of a healthy democracy is that decision-making and responsibilities are shared or distributed instead of a single micromanager. Using this concept, a husband and wife can easily delegate different responsibilities to each other. In a healthy household, children, as they grow up, learn to make appropriate decisions, and then become a part of this decision-making process. As their views are respected in the family's decision-making process, they learn to respect difference of opinion and its rewards. They learn to respectfully disagree. Another critical aspect of a democratic system is to understand and accept that once the decision-making process is over and the decision is made, everyone wholeheartedly acts on it, even those who may have differed. Unfortunately, in most families, one of the parents assumes the charge and enforces autocratic system of decision-making process. As years pass, husband and wife diverge like a fork in the road and the children are left confused, following their own directions, doubting each other, and may never reach their potential collective goal. For the society around them, the end-result is social disharmony, lack of trust, and lost opportunities for everyone.

The Odd-person Problem

We all are born with distinct physical and psychological qualities, but some of us are born with significant physical or cognitive limitations, and then there are some who are born with an exceptional trait. In the USA, a small percentage of children are born with cognitive disability, about 4%. But the number of children born with exceptional qualities is very small, about 0.0002%. Either of these occurrences create an unusual and difficult situation for the family and the society. Though both situations provide an opportunity to learn crisis management, or to achieve something exceptional, most people struggle dealing with them. This topic is quite large with multiple dimensions but my interest for the present discussion is somewhat different, I am talking about a different type of odd situation.

Sometimes, a family member, like a child, a parent, or a close relative, who otherwise may not have any obvious physical or mental disability, instead of being a useful part of the family enterprise, behaves in a manner that is destructive to the common wellbeing and goal of the family group. The whole family structure can collapse if it is one of the parents. It can also be one of the children, whose negative impact can be devastating for the psychological and financial outlook of the children and the family.

Children may show their innate personality traits in quite young age. One may experiment spending little time with any elementary school age group and easily figure out a variety of personalities. Some of those personality traits can be lifelong. Being the lead in a family, it is parents' responsibility to understand their children's personality traits and channel them accordingly. The problem arises when a child with a problematic trait is either not corrected, left alone to impact others, or the worse, is encouraged for his or her negative behavior. Not only that this type of situation affects everyone else, but the effecting child also loses the opportunity and ability to self-correct or have any realistic long-term solution of his or her problem. Like any other enterprise, sometimes, if all corrective measures fail and for the sake of collective well-being, it is better for the family to somewhat separate themselves from a problem personality or chart a separate course for that individual.

Merit vs Hierarchy

This probably is one of the fundamental issues affecting the financial outlook of developing societies. Human being is a tribal entity. A tribe can be as small as the immediate or an extended family, or an ethnicity, or a socio-political group. Some nature of favoritism exists in every society, and in some respects, it has some value. For example, individuals of a military family are more aware of the requirements and risks associated with a combat related profession. While recruiting, it can be reasonable to give some level of preference to children of a military family, but only a certain level. Not every child from a military family can be suitable for a military job either, and if an undue preference is given, the repercussions can be deadly for him or a lot many people. A military without meritocracy can never survive long enough to defend a nation.

An undue preference due to any tribal or selfish reason undermines an organization. This is one of the main differences between a society with successful enterprises from a one always struggling. Unfortunately, it is a common practice in a country like Pakistan resulting in widespread institutional ineptness and failures. Pakistanis claim to be practicing Muslims but fail to understand that the Prophet Muhammad, may peace and blessings of Allah SWT be upon him, practiced and enforced merit-based system. While picking people for a job, he was not concerned about family ties, friendships, age, or any other type of seniority or hierarchy. He appointed and promoted people based upon merit. In this manner, he exemplified true leadership.

On a family level, it is parents' responsibility to teach meritocracy to their children. If not learned at home, they may struggle with this concept all their life. For most jobs, especially in modern business enterprise, there shall never be discrimination or preference based upon gender or birth-order. Responsibilities shall be given based upon abilities, including any type of leadership. Here I recall another relevant example of Prophet Musa AS, may peace be upon him, who led his mission and his community with help of his brother Haroon (Aaron) AS. Haroon AS, who worked under guidance of Musa AS, was his elder brother, an important lesson to be learned from their account mentioned in the Quran. For a mission to be completed, the lead person should be decided based upon merit, without consideration of the birth-order.

The issue of eldest child, especially the male child, leading the family enterprise used to be a universal problem but has mostly gone out of practice in many societies.

It's origin probably was the dynastic system of national rule where the next leader was chosen based upon the birth-order. In many cases, due to incompetence of the chosen leader based upon the birth-order, a younger sibling took over the charge but usually after a bloody coup, or after sidelining or killing his own brother. As societies matured, this practice has been mostly discarded but not completely. Even now, the next person in line for the British throne is picked based upon the birth-order. In developing societies like Pakistan, this still is a significant problem though more noticeable in families with land or business resources. Repercussions of this practice can be quite harmful and continues to be a vehicle for social injustice, violation of due rights, especially of women, and lack of realistic long-term financial progress for the whole family.

A similar problem is the issue of hierarchy in government bureaucracy. Like the birth-order, sometimes people are promoted based upon their employment starting date, or age. This system, in a country like Pakistan or India, which once were under the colonial rule, might have been purposefully designed by their colonial masters. It created a perpetual system of subservient officials, both at the lower and the officer level. To their masters, it did not matter who was officiating, as they all were forced to follow orders, without any dissent. Merit and performance carried limited value and could never provide them the top-most positions.

While designing their own system, Pakistanis have kept this un-just, inept, and un-Islamic system in many places, like the judiciary. The message of Islam, based upon the practices of the Prophet Muhammad SAW, may peace be upon him, strongly favors merit or ability-based system of assigning responsibilities or promotion. If any of the private enterprise follows this practice, it also suffers just like the government.

Unjust Inheritance System

The Quran, An-Nisa, ayah 33 (Al-Quran 4:33):

> "To (benefit) everyone We have appointed shares and heirs to property left by parents and relatives. To those also to whom your right hand was pledged give their due portion: For truly Allah is Witness to all things." Ali.

> "And to everyone, We have appointed heirs of that (property) left by parents and relatives. To those also with whom you have made a pledge (brotherhood), give them their due portion (by Wasiyyah will). Truly, Allah is Ever a Witness over all things." Al-Hilali & Khan.

In an indirect manner, inheritance practices may significantly affect a society, especially its entrepreneurial activity. I divide inheritance in two types: the fixed generational assets, like the land, and relatively fluid assets, like an enterprise or a business. Legally and ethically speaking, all assets should be divided and fully transferred to their legal heirs as expeditiously as legally possible. But that requires switching control from one to another person, even if it is a brother or a sister. People do not like to give away control of assets, and they may delay it or postpone it, sometimes permanently. Women suffer much more as transferring assets to them, which is their fully legal and ethical share, is considered a loss for the family. It is not uncommon for the elder or a dominant sibling to keep full control of assets or divide them based upon his concept of fairness, not what the law may decide. Governmental probate system is weak and has very little influence to fix these financial injustices.

One of the main issues in inheritance is lack of understanding of the concept of a "will." Even though one is strongly encouraged to have a will document with clear instructions about transfer of assets, most people in a country like Pakistan do not make this arrangement. Even when wills are available, frequently they are verbal (impossible to confirm), or coerced, or plain unjust. The end-result is generational discord and financial injustice to many. People ignore the fact that as a generation gets older, the mode and ways of business may change. It is easier for the next generation to understand new ways and come up with entrepreneurial ideas in a new environment, provided they have some assets. Lack of proper transfer of inheritance stymie their economic growth and the surrounding society. To make things worse for the heirs, the legal system is extremely weak and easily corruptible.

Myopic National Policies

No nation can survive without a functional government and its associated bureaucracy, and every bureaucracy requires monetary resources to survive and to do the job it is supposed to do. Some countries are lucky to have some natural resources to sell, like oil and gas. But most governments rely on taxation to afford all the services they provide, including their own salaries and benefits. To raise more funds, the government may either collect more taxes from the same taxpayers or somehow increase the number of taxpayers while keeping the tax rate low. While there is clear evidence that the better option is the latter one, governments with poor or myopic fiscal vision opt for the former route. The second problem is of the limitation of the taxpayer base. If it is comprised mostly of government or service jobs, it seldom provides enough resources to improve a society. A healthy economy must have a broad-based tax base with a low taxation rate.

In a developing society like Pakistan, the simple concept of making the size of the economic pie bigger instead of breaking the same pie into smaller pieces is not well understood. To appease their vote base, politicians routinely add 100s to 1000s of jobs to an already saturated government departments and the so-called semi-government enterprises. No surprise that the government's budget is bloated out of bound, and enterprises are financially crippled. Public is ignorant and oblivious about basic economics. Despite witnessing and suffering from deterioration of institutions and their own quality of life, enslaved by their selfish interests including ethnic or tribal prejudices, they keep on electing the same charlatans.

What Should a Government Do Then?

A government's job is to promote entrepreneurship while keeping itself out of business enterprise. As described above, Islamic system of finance is "relatively-free" type and is market driven, not government driven. Restrictions and controls are kept at minimum as the economic outlook of a society is directly proportional to the freedom it provides for business activity. Government does what it is supposed to do, provide, implement, and support appropriate financial rules and regulations. These rules and regulations, in a country like Pakistan, can follow the fundamentals of Islam. Anything not clearly Islamic, can be restricted. The problem arises when the government makes decisions and takes steps that are clearly un-just, or against the spirit of Islamic, and then expects improvement in its financial outlook.

For a government or an establishment of a country to understand some fundamental fiscal concepts can be challenging, both in the so-called developed and less developed countries. In this regard, there are some critical economic concepts that I describe as follows:

1st concept: It is always better to expand the size of the economic pie, with respect to the size of the population, than break it into smaller pieces.

2nd concept: A self-employed citizen is always better or preferred than an employed one, whatever the nature or level of employment of the employed may be.

3rd concept: There is a level higher than the self-employed one, and that is for the one who creates and provides employment for others, an entrepreneur.

4th concept: The primary goal of a government's fiscal policies is to help and promote self-employment and entrepreneurship.

5th concept: Free or market driven economy is always better than a command or controlled economy.

6th concept: Even in a free economy, not every economic activity is beneficial for the society.

7th concept: Government, including its military, shall not be directly involved in any business activity and shall not form government or semi-government enterprises.

8th concept: No financial system can thrive or sustain without clearly established rules and regulations and a system of justice to resolve conflicts in a timely manner. This is where the government takes the lead.

9th concept: Injustices of one generation shall not become burden for the next.

10th concept: Low tax rate is always better for the economy. While some amount of taxation is needed in almost every society, higher taxes do not help the economy grow.

11th concept: Conflict-of-interest rules shall be strict and fully enforced.

12th concept: Agriculture sector may need subsidization. Food is a critical and security issue.

13th concept: Military is always a subsidized institution, but it shall never be allowed to get involved in the government or entrepreneurship.

14th concept: Central bank of the country shall be governed by an independent non-political board with one member from each province.

15th concept: Rights of disabled, orphans, and elderly shall be respected and guaranteed by the government. This include providing them with a reasonable level of sustenance.

16th concept: Entrepreneurial activities shall be balanced with their potential impact on the environment and nature. Islam does not accept injustice, even if it is done to inanimate objects.

Any society that understands these concepts and promote policies to foster self-employment and entrepreneurship may flourish and succeed. Economically failed states are ruled by foolish people who consider themselves, the people in the government, at the top and formulate policies to cater for their own interests and needs.

Conflict of Interest Issues

Probably the biggest problem with the government's approach to business, in a country like Pakistan, is either lack of understanding or willful disregard of the concept of conflict of interest. In business or in corporate world, this issue has tremendous implications. Even those whose job may be to help maintain the spirit of fairness, if not its writ, seem to either have no clue or are equally culpable.

Recently, for some reasons I stumbled upon website of the Meezan Bank, listed as the largest Islamic bank in Pakistan. The bank listed its corporate governing structure. Part of that is the so-called Sharia Board, and 2 out of the four members are a father and his son, clearly stated in that manner. Reading this detail, I was flabbergasted to say the least. I thought about its potential logical explanation. One possibility is that they may have ownership in this enterprise. But if that is the case, it may create even a larger conflict of interest. Another possibility is that they are not aware of either the subject of conflict of interest or the notion that having two close relatives in the board can create such problem. Though logically possible, this explanation is implausible, because both the father and his son are well educated in Islamic law, modern jurisprudence, and experienced in corporate governance. Unfortunately, the logical explanations I could come up was that either they consider themselves above these rules, or they have a fundamental misunderstanding or lack of understanding of what fairness and Islamic law is. To my surprise, to make things worse, Meezan Bank is a public company, not private. I really doubt if this type of fiasco will be tolerated or approved by any other society or its shareholders.

Somehow people do not understand that each board member in the Sharia board must make his or her own decision about any product or question brought to them by the bank's administrative board. Because, if they do not, it will be a disservice on their part. Do the overseeing authorities do not see that putting a father and son, even if they both were individually or distinctly qualified for the job, has created a conflict of interest for each one of them. On the bank's website, there is no mention of their portfolio, their manner of making decisions, or their compensation, which should also be looked at. They have not listed their other appointments either, which could easily create further conflict of interest.

Another common example of the issue of conflict of interest in Pakistan is the issue of land acquisition by its official elites. Probably, the most precious commodity for a common Pakistani is a plot of land to build a house, which in an extremely populated country is not cheap, and the most expensive one is in the capital. It is quite a routine that a government department will formulate an association to obtain land for housing for its members. Army, especially its officer class, is particularly good at it. None of them understand that they all are abusing their official positions and inflicting a financial harm to the rest of the society, which is a particularly abusive form of *Riba*. They were not hired by the people of Pakistan to use their official positions to benefit themselves. They were hired to help solve people's problems, including housing. Instead of building a fair system of affordable housing for everyone, all they have created is an extremely unfair practice tilted to their own interests. Again, like the example provided above, people have no understanding of the conflict of interest, or they are willfully ignoring it.

What Governing Structure is Best For a corporation?

Like the above-described different types of economies, there also are different types of management systems or styles. Probably the oldest and still the most prevalent system of leadership is autocratic, in which one person makes all or almost all decisions. It is commonly practiced on a family level when a parent, usually a man, enforces his leadership role. Sometimes, it is the other way around and the mother is in charge. Example of an autocratic style of governance for a business is sole proprietorship where one person starts or is in full control of the business. This is a common and expected practice for most startups, but as the nature of business is getting more and more technological and complicated, even startups may start with more than one person in-charge. I try to explain this issue by dividing it in different types of business situations:

    A. Sole ownership or sole entrepreneurship: Every enterprise or a business starts with an idea, and the best of those starts with a new idea or a new way of something others might have already been doing. A sole owner must come up with the idea, formulate a plan for execution, execute and troubleshoot, and keep on doing it every day of the week. Entrepreneurship is not a 9 to 5 job; it is a 24/7 commitment. Sole entrepreneurs are also the backbone of any financial system, constantly creating new ideas while keeping people employed. In a society like Pakistan, sole ownership is mostly for traders (like shop owners), or service professionals (like barbers and doctors). Socio-legal and political environment is less conducive for innovation-oriented entrepreneurship.

B. Family enterprise: Family enterprise is more than just a business. It becomes a legacy and a source of pride for the family. Emotional attachment of owners to such business is an asset but it can easily become a liability too. Once successful, probably the most difficult and urgent task for a family business owner is to formulate a proper succession plan, which may keep the business flourishing while keeping it in family's control. They need to make this decision without any prejudice (e.g., birth order, gender) and as early as possible. It takes time to couch and groom a leader. Every situation can be different, some may just require designation of the next leader while others may need to establish a board of directors. All these arrangements have one thing in common, the owner must let go of the control, even if partially or slowly. Another reason to take care of this responsibility is the nature of Islamic laws of inheritance, which, at minimum, require timely transfer of appropriate shares to each child, of every gender, and all other heirs. This may be easier to accomplish while the first generation, especially the founder, is living and in control.

C. Large private company: Every company starts from a small business, which may become larger family business, and ultimately a large company. Some of it is discussed above. The issue of a large private company is somewhat more complicated than a family enterprise, as it may or may not be a family enterprise. Probably the most important issues at this level are two: a. Clear understanding of the mission of the enterprise, and b. Well defined governing structure with its rules and regulations. These issues are important for every enterprise, but they need to be clearly elaborated as the company size reach a certain level. As far as what is the definition of a small or a large company, it can be different in different societies. At this stage of an enterprise, it may not be possible for one person to be fully versed with all aspects of the business. It may have multiple divisions with multiple people involved. It is the leadership's role to set direction, stay focused, assign responsibilities, and establish a system of accountability, including for the board running the show.

D. Public company: The main difference between a large private company and a public company is the transparency. While a large private company may not have to declare their governing structures, a public company shall not hide any details. The mission and the governing structure must be clear, as described above for a large private company. As a public company accepts large number of people, in fact anyone, as their partners, they have a moral and fiscal responsibility to be completely forthcoming and clear about their mission, plans, and their management.

E. Not-for-profit enterprises: The definition of these enterprises and the laws governing them may vary in every society, and every such company must be versed and compliant with these laws. In a way, everything stated above may also apply to this type of enterprise. Their mission must be clear and transparent, their governing structure well defined, and they must have a clearly established system of accountability and conflict resolution. If done in a proper manner, it may flourish, and nurtured by the community. If on the other hand, any aspect of it is murky, despite its non-profit status, the society may easily discard it.

Corporate governance is also influenced by local customs and traditions. For example, typical British corporate governance is more tradition and custom based, in comparison to the American model, which is more regulation based. One may find same types of differences in their political structures and governance. Countries affected by the British system, including its previous Muslim colonies, are following somewhat same systems. Reviewing the details of Islamic finance, as elaborated in previous chapters, one may say that the Islamic system of corporate governance is in fact closer to American type than the British type, as it is more of a regulation-based system instead of tradition based.

The Financial Goldmine

Allah SWT awards and rewards people based upon His will and wisdom. Some individuals or a society can be given resources without any of their own efforts. An individual may inherit large number of resources, or a country may discover something underground to sell. In either case, they may own a large sum of resources with limited effort of their own, which is different from what is the case for most people in the world. In day-to-day financial jargon, one may call it a financial goldmine. As per Islamic understanding, every opportunity or resource given, or not given, to an individual or a nation, is a trial. It can be a source of great blessing or a never-ending misery or discord, depending how it is managed. It is not uncommon to find people destroying their ancestral wealth in a matter of months to years, and not every country with oil & gas to export is rich, progressing, and peaceful. Governance, and in this case, proper corporate governance is the key that determines their fate, their success or failure in the test Allah SWT conferred upon them.

Chapter 17

The Conclusion

I hope that I was able to provide some basic information to anyone trying to research Islamic way of business or finance. A large part of the book was dedicated to the basic knowledge about Islam, which was intentional for anyone not fully familiar with this subject. It was not my intention to represent any sect or a school of thought. This, I believe, is important for the upcoming generations of Muslims in both Muslim and non-Muslim societies. For the same reason though, it might not have gone well within certain people, or the communities more interested in their way of understanding, teaching, or practice, instead of the basic spirit of Islam.

Some might disapprove the overall perspective of this writing, especially the reasoning and the search for logically best answers. Unfortunately, it is not uncommon to hear that the Islam and the "logic" or "reasoning with logic" are not synonymous, if not mutually exclusive.

This is an important misconception to address but not the topic of this work. In brief, the message of Allah SWT is far from it. Human being is particularly bestowed to observe, read, reflect, reason and understand. While challenging the logical analysis on one hand, and not fully understanding the limitations, some people misconstrue humans' lack of full understanding to any understanding at all. The logical way to find an answer to a question, after appropriate research, is to review all possible solutions and come up with the best, as outlined in the Quran:

The Quran, Az-Zumar, *ayah* 18 (Al-Quran 39:18):

> "Those who listen to the Word, and follow the best (meaning) in it: those are the ones whom Allah has guided, and those are the ones endured with understanding." Ali.

> "Those who listen to the Word [good advice *La ilaha ill Allah* – (none has the right to be worshipped but Allah) and Islamic Monotheism etc.] and follow the best thereof (i.e., worship Allah Alone, repent to Him and avoid *Taghut*, etc.) those are (the ones) whom Allah has guided and those are men of understanding (like Zaid bin 'Amr bin Nufail, Salman Al-Farsi and Abu-Dhar Al-Ghafari)." Al-Hilali & Khan.

This is by no means an all-comprehensive book about Islamic finance and the *Riba*. I hope that it will trigger further research and writings, but more importantly, actions, on the part of individuals and the Muslim societies, to help improve their financial outlook by following the guidelines mentioned in the Quran and approved by the Prophet Muhammad SAW.

The Quran, Ar-Ra'd, *ayah* 11 (Al-Quran 13:11):

> "... Verily never will Allah change the condition of a people until they change it themselves ... " Ali.

> "... Allah will not change the good condition of a people as long as they do not change their state of goodness themselves ... " Al-Hilali & Khan.

Finance and Islamic jurisprudence, both are complex subjects with their multiple applications. Someone critical of this work may easily find a flaw or many in this writing, but it is difficult to ignore a lot many areas that are relatively straight-forward or non-controversial but still require a lot of our attention. Some may call this effort a Western influenced discourse. Though, the concept of the East and the West is an arbitrary one. Islam is neither Western nor Eastern, it is a global and universal religion. Every Muslim in the world is trying or should be trying and struggling to be on the right path. Allah SWT requires us to continue this struggle, as the purpose of life is nothing but this struggle. Its success, in both material and the spiritual contexts, depends at least upon staying on the recommended path. May Allah SWT help us to not waver from it. Amen.

Finally, thinking of a unifying concept around all the rules and regulations about finance or trade, based upon the Quran and the *Sunnah* of the Prophet SAW, the basic requirement is to do justice, and avoid injustice. If a trader is selling rice at a price of a dollar a pound and deliver the exact five pounds of rice with a charge of $5, he is doing justice, which is the basic and fundamental Islamic requirement. A Muslim trader may never deliver any amount less than 5 pounds, an act of injustice if it happens, and shall rather consider adding an ounce or two, an act of *Ihsaan*, knowing that Allah SWT does not like injustice. HE recommends justice, but above all, He, the *Al-Adl* (the Just) and the *Al-Kareem* (the Generous), loves those who do better and stay on the side of *Ihsaan*. As for those in-charge or the government, their mission shall be establishment of justice and prevention of injustice.

References:

1. Al-Muwatta of Imam Malik bin Anas, translated by Aisha Abdurrahman Bewley. Diwan Press 2014, United Kingdom.

2. Sahih Al-Bukhari, translated by Hilal Yayinlari, Crescent Publishing House, Turkey, 2nd Edition, 1976.

3. Sahih Al-Bukhari, translated by Dr. Muhammad Muhsin Khan, Darussalam, Kingdom of Saudi Arabia, 1997.

4. Sahih Muslim, translated by Nasiruddin al-Khattab, Darussalam, 2007.

5. Musnad Imam Ahmad bin Hambal, translated by Nasiruddin al-Khattab, Darussalam, 2012.

6. Sunan ibn Majah, translated by Nasiruddin al-Khattab, Darussalam, 2007.

7. Sunan Abu Dawud, translated by Nasiruddin al-Khattab, Darussalam, 2008.

www.ingramcontent.com/pod-product-compliance
Lightning Source LLC
Chambersburg PA
CBHW071350210526
45465CB00001B/51